AMONG OTHER THINGS

Robert Long Foreman

AMONG OTHER THINGS

PLEIADES
PRESS

Lena-Miles Wever Todd Poetry Series
Warrensburg, Missouri

Library of Congress Control Number:
ISBN: 978-0-8071-6661-1

Published by Pleiades Press

Department of English
University of Central Missouri
Warrensburg, Missouri 64093

Distributed by Louisiana State University Press

Cover Image: Amy Bennett, "Up to Our Necks." Oil on panel, 6 x 6.

Book design by Sarah Nguyen
Author's photo by Stefanie Wortman
First Pleiades Printing, 2017

Financial support for this project has been provided by a HILO grant
from the University of Central Missouri and the Missouri Arts Council,
a state agency.

for my mother and

in memory of Miles

Table of Contents

PREFACE

It is very hard to write a good essay. I always knew that.

I gained a new appreciation for the genre's difficulty when I returned, recently, to writing essays after five years of writing short stories and a novel.

I wrote nothing but essays, mostly of the personal variety, for six years prior to the turn to fiction. For those years it was familiar ground. It was all I knew, as a writer, and so I expected the doubling back to essays to feel something like coming home, or putting on a shirt I used to enjoy but haven't seen in a long time, maybe because I had changed my mind about shirts.

It wasn't like that at all. The road to the genre I had thought of as home, all along, had grown over. The shirt had developed three new sleeves and I didn't know which sleeves to put my arms through.

I don't know what it was that really changed. Maybe nothing changed, and it's only that by estranging myself from the essay for so long I lost sight of just what a daunting thing it can be to write one. That's probably it.

The difference isn't only that when writing a short story the writer has something more to hide behind, like in many cases a fictional narrator who wholly, or nearly wholly, supplants, and doesn't merely supplement, the representation of the writer.

It is also that the essay has a trajectory all its own. Whereas a short story might well proceed in a straight line, an essay will generally not. It is more likely to go in circles, until it gives up on the circles and crisscrosses over itself in the hope that even though it isn't going far something will be dug or built up in the course of its retreading.

When done well, the result appears effortless, but in my experience it is a uniquely maddening thing to bring into being.

Most of the essays in this book were written prior to my escape into writing fiction, an escape that took place in Indiana, at a cabin on the coast of Lake Michigan. I hadn't known the coast of Lake Michigan could be found in Indiana, and I had no intention when I went there to start doing anything new. My wife, Stefanie, and I wanted to be in a place with scenery and few domestic demands, someplace where we could clear our heads and breathe and take long walks beside a pretty lake big enough to drown in and not be found again.

Beside our cabin was a stable, and in the stable lived horses we made up names for: Whiteface, Kneesocks, Whitey and Black Beauty. An orange cat would come around. We called him Tough Guy, for he would sit on a fencepost and seem to keep watch over the other animals, who were many times his size.

One horse we called Frosted Doughnut, because he looked more like a frosted doughnut than the other horses did. He was a nervous horse, or so he seemed to me—I, who have spent no time with horses. He stood in a tiny pen he never seemed to leave and chewed hay that was stacked around him on all sides. He was a rescue horse, we learned, not in the sense that he came to the rescue but in that he had been rescued, from a neglectful prior owner, I assumed.

I was supposed to be working on what would become the next-to-last essay in this collection. Instead I drank a lot of coffee and sat on the cabin porch, across the yard from Frosted Doughnut. Stefanie was inside, revising the manuscript for her first book of poems, and I didn't work on anything until the end of the week, when I started writing my first short story. It didn't have any horses in it.

Although we invented our own names for them, Tough Guy, Frosted Doughnut, Kneesocks and the other horses did exist. I have similarly renamed certain human beings portrayed in this book, for their protection as much as mine, but, like the horses, they are or were at one time alive, or so the evidence of memory and text would attest. Scenes in the essays that follow have been rendered as faithfully to objective truth as possible, and every sentence was written with the intent to portray things with clarity and honesty. The value of clarity, honesty, and objective truth is a worthy subject for another preface to a different book.

SPEAK, WALKING STICK

I got poison ivy seven times one summer. The third bout was my worst: it crept up into my face and itched, and itched. I applied calamine lotion in thick layers under my left eye and down my neck, underneath my shirt. As I walked about town I saw people I knew, waved and said hello, told them why my face was oozing and laughed. I was not avoiding people for no reason, as I often did. I was making eye contact. The calamine lotion somehow placed me better socially—put a safe obstruction between my face and another person's.

More recently, I inherited a walking stick. I picked it up at random, during a stay at my parents' house. It rested on a cane rack that came from my great-aunt Catherine when she died. As I paced about the dining room I picked up the stick nonchalantly, as I might snatch up a pen to chew on when I get restless. The stick filled my momentary need to hold onto something. It appeared exactly when and where I needed it, and once I was through with pacing, I gave it the thorough estimation a thing of its character is due.

As pieces of wood go, it was beautiful: dark, slender, and gnarly. Its color was a deep brown that verged on black and suggested it was once amber but turned evil. Heavier than it looked, it stretched the length of my leg from a crooked point to its bulbous grip. A sliver of it was chipped out near the middle, likely many years before. It bore a polished appearance, despite its backwoods feel. Its shape expressed its

13

longevity, the years having bent it slightly. When gripped from its shape-ly head, or balanced at its middle, it felt like a loose appendage. It would have made an excellent weapon, had things ever come to that.

A walking stick sounds like an awfully pretentious thing to car-ry around everywhere—does anyone really need one outside of a forest? I worried about this question for a short while, until I really considered the appearance of this particular walking stick. It had no plated handles, whether ivory, gold, or even plastic. It was wooden, and quite abrasively so. It was a rude walking stick. It was rustic in a way I had never quite managed to be, despite my hailing from a state that is widely considered so. It was the stick of a man who worked hard, who carried austerity in his bones—as well as in the wooden club gripped between his fingers.

I may not be especially austere, but the stick made up for that. It challenged my introspection. It answered my benign complexion with a muted harshness. I could have clutched it in my hand as I froze to death in an alley in a Charles Dickens novel, and felt appropriate.

My mother grew excited and began praising the stick as soon as she saw me with the walking stick. Since her aunt Catherine died, she had taken up the task of talking about long-dead relatives as soon as she was prompted. She knew what cousin of which ancestor was a drunk; she knew how tall they both were and where went all of the money they had back then.

The walking stick belonged to my great-grandfather, a Cum-mins who played the fiddle at church and loved Edgar Allan Poe, who walked four times over the Wheeling Suspension Bridge each day and most likely brought the stick with him when he did.

My mother has spoken about his daily walking habits since I was a child. He would wake in the morning and march to work. He would later return home, the same way, over the bridge. He would again cross the Ohio River for a newspaper, and back once more. This habit, my mother often speculated, may have been what kept him alive for more than ninety years.

I could see why it might have kept him out of danger. The walking stick was a pedestrian's first line of defense. When I held it at a proper angle, with the more substantial weight toward its head, I could not imagine a better use for it than to bludgeon something. The stick would have served poorly as a cane, reaching just short of the ground and lacking the proper grip to be one. It would have proven ideal for beating away stray dogs, or stray children. I was no more likely to start a cudgeling rampage than I had been the day before I found the stick, but just as holding a pistol for the first time must evoke thoughts of gunning people down—whether in horror or anticipation— the stick evoked the same violent speculation, mostly of the leery variety.

I carry a pen wherever I go, because I often write things down. I carry a wallet to facilitate my consumer behaviors. The walking stick identified me as a pedestrian. It served me as a prop more than as an essential tool. It was a thing I could rely on to complement myself— something by which others could recognize me. If I were to walk with it consistently, I thought, I would cease to be thought of as the guy who walks with his neck arched slightly back, or the young man who dresses in a way that isn't remarkable. I would be the guy with the walking stick.

When, after first discovering it, I thought of venturing out with the walking stick, I felt as though I contemplated going outside, anywhere, for the first time in my life. I relived some of the pivotal moments from my fifteenth year. I had spent much of my time until then indoors, more than I imagine most people did. I ate terribly, was generally unfriendly and resentfully secluded. I rarely spoke, and hardly knew what my own face looked like. Worst of all, when from my parents' house I pictured the next street over my mind drew a blank. I could not conceive of experience beyond that house and the building where I went to high school.

The obsessive habit of walking changed that, and once I started I began then to look in the mirror and discover that I had facial expressions. I ceased to sleep fully clothed. I spoke to people. When my walking habit began, I faced an incredible degree of fear and sadness when I so much as approached the door. It was a bold move for me at the time to walk outside, and with a walking stick in my hand, I thought, I might feel the same paranoia, the same hundreds of eyes on me as before, none of which were ever there. I would stick out like a sore thumb, but one that is wrapped around a very conspicuous ornament, which people may very likely scoff at and mock me for carrying.

I once felt the same way about wearing a green shirt, which I felt made me much more noticeable and therefore a likely object of ridicule about town.

Like a green shirt, the walking stick could start to feel something like a part of me—maybe an unnecessary part of me, as though I had a tail, but no less a constituent part. When I carried it, someone would occasionally shout "faggot" at me from a passing car, but then that would be no different from when I was fifteen. Inevitably people would laugh at me and my walking stick, or think I was trying for special attention, and glare. All the while, as they walked in tight crowds or cruised past in automobiles, I would be the one with a pointed, blunt object in my hand.

Friends, I thought, would question my need for a walking stick. When they asked me why I carried it, I would tell them it offered a certain stability, or companionship, that calmed me somehow. I had never wanted a steady walking partner who spoke, and the stick fulfilled a need for silent company.

I would be stronger with the walking stick at my side. I would be prepared. I was a committed pedestrian, and this evidence of it would most likely outlast me. The stick would complete my walking self when I had not realized that I was a fragment.

CLUBS

On the floor of my living room, next to my favorite bookshelf, is a piece of wood I bought at an antique mall in Canonsburg, Pennsylvania, four years ago. It is just over two feet long and thicker at its top than at its handle, which is broken off; its absent lower half resides in the trunk of my car. It is covered with nicks and cuts that resemble a child's teeth marks. It smells like porch furniture.

When I first saw the piece of wood, when it was whole, in Canonsburg, I thought it was a severed bed post. It didn't look like anything else I'd seen, but then it seemed thick for a bed post, and someone had tied on the handle a tag that read "Club $8."

The club was as blunt as an object could be, and heavy. In the right hands it could break bones, I thought, or at least cause a substantial bruise on an arm or a leg. I decided not to buy it. Instead I drove to Pittsburgh, where I lived with my brother Jim, and worked in the office of a company that packaged peaches and dog food.

For weeks I thought about the club, and regretted having left it at the shop. I didn't want to use it; I hadn't hit someone with an object since, as a child, I had gotten into fights with Jim. Rather, it was a novel artifact, a curiosity. I wanted to have the club simply because I couldn't stop thinking about it, and I wanted to see it again, up close, and hold it in my hands.

I returned to the Canonsburg antique shop, found the club

where I had left it, and walked it to the counter, where two clerks snickered and watched me like I might have a problem. One of them said, "Hey, what do you think you need this for?" I told him there was a seal in my backyard, and we laughed together. I didn't really have a backyard. One of the men wrapped the club in brown paper, to make it less brazen wherever I took it, but that only seemed to make it more conspicuous, like it meant admitting the club was indeed a weapon, a thing that deserves to be hidden.

~

Clubs are found most commonly not in antique stores but in the possession of police officers. The clubs they carry are made of metal, and are sold to the public by private companies with badly designed web sites. A variety of club often seen on the belt of an officer, the "side handle" baton, is shaped like an unfinished H; it resembles an old-fashioned club, but has an extra handle coming off one side. Its design grew popular in the wake of the Civil Rights Movement, when clubs had garnered a bad reputation. Clubs had been used in plain sight to bludgeon activists, rather than to halt thieves and killers, so the nightstick reinvented itself. It grew an extra handle, like a disguise. Its purpose stayed the same, though, and so did the ones who were paid to wield them.

~

When I brought my club home, I leaned it against a doorframe. There were no overt threats to my safety, so rather than use the club for self-defense I sometimes picked it up absentmindedly and paced the living room. I would swing it gently at my side or cradle it in my arm or hold it leaning on my shoulder like a cat. The club would end up underneath a chair, and I would roll it with my feet as I read books.

The club didn't look menacing, in my hands, when I held it in front of a mirror. If I gripped it like it was a baseball bat, or like I was a warrior primate, it was clear from the way my hands didn't properly wrap around it that I had never played baseball, or defended a primitive dwelling from Cro-Magnon interlopers. I might as well have tried to convincingly wield a lightning bolt.

18

A safe way to witness the use of clubs is to watch footage of police beatings. One film, available online, is of the brutal apprehension of Michael Cephus, from the fourth of July, 2008, in New York City. In the clip, for nearly two full minutes, one officer holds Cephus' arms against his body, as he lies on the pavement, while another batters his legs with a club, swinging his arm high and dropping the cudgel against the man's bare shins. The club's impact is audible, and it is the worst sound I have heard in months. Cephus shrieks from the pain, an off-camera onlooker screams as she watches, and another person holds the camera steady, somehow.

The club in use against Cephus is not a side handle baton; it appears to be a retractable club, like the one that can be bought from a web site called "Knives Deal" for $14.99. I have seen a demonstration film of this club. In it, a man with white hair subdues a series of attackers in the graffiti-stricken ruin of what looks like an elementary school. With the club he chokes someone. He bats the wrist of another man, who then drops the knife in his hand. The film is bold and action-packed, a marketing tool that implies that clubs are meant for use against violent gangs and men with sharp weapons, rather than those who drink too much and misbehave on national holidays.

~

At a museum somewhere, in my early twenties, I saw a collection of weapons on display behind glass. They were ancient, and had likely been used for killing people—possibly Europeans. A long metal cudgel had a five-inch spike stemming off it that could have punctured a skull, if swung with enough vigor. I watched it and thought of this for so long that I gave myself a headache. There were paintings at the museum, and sculptures and other gorgeous things, but it would have been hard for someone to penetrate my brain with them—at least physically—so they didn't make quite the impression the weapon did. The spiked, metal, murderous tool reclined against the display like a stock-still anaconda. I was reluctant to tear myself away from it, in a way my friend, an art

19

history student, could not relate to.

My own club held the same provocative mystery. It wasn't stained with blood and brains, but I wondered if it had been put to use by previous owners. It was nicked all over, so something had once been done with it—there was no telling what.

As long as I owned the club, though, I knew it wasn't being used for the thing it was supposed to be used for. Because I possessed it, no one was being struck with it to initiate a mugging. It wasn't being used to discipline a dog. I bought the club because I thought it seemed interesting. As a happy side effect, I kept it from the hands of someone who might think it seemed useful.

~

A surprising number of violent confrontations between cops and non-cops that can be seen online do not involve the use of clubs. From what I have seen, in the heat of excessive force, at least when they know it's being filmed, and they don't use their guns, officers often forego the tools at their belts and instead resort to fighting with their fists and feet, or they shove and pull their targets to the ground with their hands.

This was not the case, famously, when the police pulled over Rodney King. Until recently, I had not committed the necessary minute and sixteen seconds to watching the complete 1991 film of men from the LAPD clubbing him. I had seen short clips of the brutal scene on TV, but the full tape, as I suspected, is far worse—second after second of eerily silent mayhem, a team of uniformed trolls exacting an inebriate's impromptu retribution. With its quiet it invites meditation, but depicts a scene that is nearly unwatchable. The film demonstrates what clubs are made for, the unfortunate purpose they are all—even mine—meant to serve.

When the police brutalized King, they used side handle batons. It is hard to tell from the grainy film that the clubs have handles on their sides, but reports are specific on this point.

There is also an Internet message board on which someone claims that the side handle is useless, or at least insufficient for a policeman's purpose, and that the King beating made plain the side handle's shortcomings. But from what I have seen, the club did exactly what it

20

was meant to. In the film, after repeated strokes of the side handle, King ultimately sprawls prostrate, and in his mugshot he looks like he has been mauled by a concrete mixer.

When I bought my club, I thought I had found a unique treasure—one small but telling piece of our world, an expression of the nation we inhabit, a vessel of misery at rest, suspended while I had it between owners potentially more violent than I. But instead it was one club among millions, and some of its brothers were in the wrong hands.

~

I went to visit my parents in Wheeling, and my mother told me I should look at something my father had in his bedroom. She said it was an old, wooden club. She didn't know I had been writing about my club, and I don't think she knew I owned it.

I went searching through my father's bedroom and found his club between two bookshelves. It looked ceremonial: short and wooden, an ornate ring was carved around its handle, with divots punched in it.

My mother told me my paternal great-grandfather had owned the club, because he volunteered for a fire department, in northern West Virginia. That didn't make sense—firefighters carry hoses and axes—but I didn't question it. Then my father admitted that although his grandfather had fought fires, the club had served a different purpose. He had also been an active member of the Ku Klux Klan.

This was not news to me; my parents had mentioned it many times before. Nearly the only thing I know about my father's grandfather is that he was a domestic terrorist, and that as soon as he died my great-grandmother burned his robe.

My mother used to reassure me that this doesn't mean I come from bad people, that if you lived, as my ancestor did, in the middle of nowhere, and many of your friends were in the Klan, it was something you could get involved in without comprehending its import. She has said that, for many in the region of my birth, the Klan was like a social club, like a college fraternity without a college. As it happens, this is precisely the way a family friend once described to me the police department he worked in, the night I drove him to the funeral of one of his colleagues.

My mother has also told me, half-joking, that there were so few African-Americans in northern West Virginia at the same time as my great-grandfather, the Klan would have spent their time harassing Catholics.

People in my family today are well aware of what the Klan is about, and none of us are members. I had always considered this part of our history to be bygone and irrelevant, something that had been disposed of with the flowing, white robe my great-grandmother so promptly disintegrated, but here, in the club, was evidence of that history, which had survived her effort at cleaning the family up.

I had thought my club from Canonsburg was suspect and weird. I had worried that a previous wielder might have used it to harm someone. But in the case of this other club, this Klansman's tool, it seemed safe to assume that someone had put it to use, and had done it gladly. It would have been made not to stop rapists, but to bludgeon Papists and African-Americans. It would have been used by my father's mother's father, someone I never met, but who shares with me some essential traits; we might even have identical hands.

It was hard to know exactly what to make of the wooden club, as I lay it on my father's bed and stared at it. The thing was unsuspecting enough; it didn't even look dangerous. Yet it represented what is likely the worst component of my lineage, an insidious piece of my ancestry. I felt glad I had bought my own club in Canonsburg. It meant another truncheon was in the family now, with a previous owner unknown. Its meaning was mine to determine, and I had a new reason to be relieved that it was broken into several useless fragments.

~

Some police batons are sold with the guarantee that they cannot be broken. Baton manufacturer ASP claims that its products "have an incredible psychological deterrence and unparalleled control potential." I don't know what that means, but the literature also states that, "Tested by the most elite federal teams, the ASP Baton has proven itself 'virtually indestructible,'" so that a purchaser will know that the club in his hand will not break and fail him in a desperate moment, when someone tries to stab him in an alley at midnight, or when he encounters a drunken man in broad daylight next Independence Day.

When the ASP product information claims that their baton is "the finest impact weapon produced," their copywriters mean it. Their clubs are made with an unflagging readiness to hurt. They are made to bring suffering, and not the hardest of skulls, shins or shoulders will stand in their way.

~

I tried to use my club only once, when I went to a park with some friends. The club was in my trunk. When a blonde guy I didn't know ventured to his car and retrieved a baseball, I could not resist; I went to my car, brought out the club, and suggested we use it as a bat. People liked the club, and thought it was a funny thing. Then we started playing.

I made contact with the ball on the first pitch, but as soon as the two objects met in mid-swing the weight in my hand got suddenly lighter. Still gripping the handle, I watched its thick business end go hurtling across the field and land in the grass. The club's most important half, its focus point of bad potential energy, broke off and spun away from me.

I was stunned. All along, the club had not been dangerous. It had been a fraud—a useless slice of wood, a waste of tree.

I don't know how to recognize different types of wood, except cherry, so I couldn't say what the club was made of. Its insides resembled Styrofoam. I was lucky to have never used it for self-defense after all, or for assaulting someone, as I would then have looked even sillier.

I reacted to the death of the club with a mixture of surprise, embarrassment, and relief. Clearly it could not be used to harm someone; it was broken, and had never been strong enough to be useful in a fight, or in a future owner's spell of drunken rage. I wondered if it had not been a club after all. I gathered its broken pieces and walked them to my car. I have not tried to put it back together.

CARLO

Once or twice a year, I suffer through a nightmare in which, due to a grievous clerical oversight, I am sent back to high school to fulfill neglected credit hours. It doesn't matter that I've gone to college and have a Master's degree. I inhabit once again the poorly lit hallways and classrooms of the college preparatory school in which I spent four years of my youth. Again I must answer to the faculty who were, when I attended the first time, as nonplussed as I was by a rhombus, and who were more eager to coach and fraternize with runners and swimmers than they were to teach me to diagram a sentence, a task the value of which I was just smart enough to question at the time. At night, asleep, I despair at the hours of homework that lie ahead of me, the people I must answer to, and my very location.

The location is West Virginia, and I am reluctant to use the name of the school where my bad dreams take place, as it is still operational, my account of it could be mistaken for libel, and the school's administrators could send lawyers after me. It would be a fate worse than having to take more classes there, so rather than use the school's actual name, I will call it Carlo, after Emily Dickinson's pet Newfoundland.

Carlo was founded in 1814, as was stipulated by the will of a lawyer from Connecticut who had settled in the region. He was once quoted as saying, "Go forth and no retreat," though it is unclear to whom he was speaking at the time. His namesake school began as a

Lancastrian academy, deploying a system of education invented in England at the turn of the nineteenth century, in which students, upon being taught a lesson, were asked to teach the same lesson to their peers. Upstart Lancastrian students were sometimes tied up in sacks, or suspended from a classroom ceiling in a cage, but neither this strange discipline nor the peer education system were practiced at Carlo, at least not by the time I arrived. Such austerity toward the students would not have gone over well, as Carlo depended—and still depends—for its survival on the voluntary attendance of students, more particularly on their parents' tuition payments.

Nestled among Appalachian hills, with a parking lot full of cars, some of them fancy and driven by teenagers, the school is expensive. A handful of students from families with modest incomes were able to attend on athletic scholarships, and the school had its share of middle-class attendees, but Carlo was known for being the city's haven for wealthy kids. This was not an undeserved reputation, and stories that illustrated the students' significant wealth circulated freely. One night in the tenth grade, my classmate Terence Lazlo, both of whose parents were doctors, wrecked his brand new SUV while driving drunk. He was unharmed. Weeks later, his parents bought him another brand new SUV.

With an enrollment of just over 400 students, Carlo is dwarfed by the city's public school, which stands on a taller, more crowded hill a few miles away, out of sight. Still, Carlo has a sizable campus, with an impressive field house, dormitories for the boarding students, and houses, owned by the school, where the teachers live. All of the classes are held in still another building, one with deeply red bricks and windows tinted as dark as the windows of Terence Lazlo's SUVs.

Next to this main building is an old gymnasium. Beside the gymnasium, when I attended, were some bushes and a pit filled with vines, and among the vines was the barrel of an artillery piece from the Civil War. Curious students would go, after school, to visit the cannon among the greenery. They would lift its front end and marvel at its heft. I would join them, and insist that the cannon had once belonged to my grandfather.

It was true. My mother's father was a doctor and historian of field artillery weapons of the Civil War—he co-authored a book on the subject, *Field Artillery Weapons of the Civil War*. Having attended Carlo, he most likely donated money to the school. I know for a fact that he gave it a cannon; my elder brothers had explained to me many times, with pride, that the cannon in Carlo's yard had once been our patriarch's, not unlike the cannons in our living room that he had left to us. My mother, on the other hand, had forgotten about the cannon, had she ever been aware of it. Years after my years at Carlo, she learned that a man unaffiliated with the school had discovered the piece of ordnance, and was planning to restore and even fire it for his own amusement. At first she was indignant, but after meeting the enthusiast and deciding he did not have questionable plans for the artillery, she approved of his plan. She had, however, been furious to learn that her father's gift to the school had been sitting under vines in a pit for something like twenty years; I remember her saying, "Someone gives them a cannon, and they throw it in the yard? Jesus!"

I did not, like all of my five siblings, graduate from Carlo. Instead, in the eleventh grade, I departed it to attend the nearest public one. Because of this, I rendered myself slightly different from the others in my family. I found a way out of their common experience. When my eldest brother Sam, at a recent family reunion, praised the pedagogy of Mr. Price, the senior-level English teacher, I was the only one among my four brothers and one sister who could not judge whether Sam's enthusiasm was misplaced, as I had not lasted long enough to sit in Price's classroom. I didn't have to disagree with Sam; I had no opinion on the matter. This was a small dose of bliss for me.

I did not graduate from Carlo, but for four years I acquiesced to tradition and my parents' wishes. I let Carlo dictate the content of my mornings and afternoons, the friends I would meet, the books I would read, and the temperature of the pasta salad I would eat, or choose not to eat, in its lunchroom. I also let Carlo dictate, for the rest of my life, the landscape of some of my most unpleasant dreams—though to say I let it do this is misleading, as I was forced to go. When I was twelve, my parents dragged me one morning to the main building, where I was made to take an admissions exam and meet briefly with the headmaster. I was being evaluated as a potential student, but it was a formality; I suspect I could have done anything short of pissing on the floor and I would have been admitted, as the school officials knew my family well, and probably couldn't afford to turn away any students, let alone one with two younger siblings who were likely to also attend there.

As much as I hated the public school, where I was in danger of failing math and I mourned every miserable day, I didn't want to go to Carlo, in large part because of the socioeconomic status of so many of its attendees. I didn't want to be associated with all of that wealth, for reasons I could not have explained had I tried.

I may have been embarrassed by what I perceived as my own family's prosperity. I thought, when I first entered Carlo, that we must have been moderately wealthy, even if our fortunes didn't match those of the families of other students. We weren't poor; my father was a lawyer, and we lived in a sizable house with inherited antiques to spare. Starting, however, sometime toward the end of the seventh grade, my mother hinted on occasion that we were not as comfortable as appearances suggested. One night she told me that my father had to take out loans so that I could attend Carlo, and that he had done the same for my three elder brothers. My parents were in debt, on my behalf, and immediately I felt the weight of it on my shoulders. I think my mother meant, by giving me this information, to make me conscious of the expensive things in my life that I might take for granted and shouldn't. It worked, perhaps better than she intended.

Soon after that conversation, I stumbled onto one of Carlo's tuition bills. It was on our kitchen table. It wasn't meant for me, but with a curious glance I saw that a year there cost my parents seven thousand dollars.

The amount was—to me—staggering. I had never thought the tuition could be so high, and now that a definite figure was attached to my education, I could not get it out of my head. I thought, every chance I had to think it, as I was lectured to on postulates, and as I filled out flash cards with vocabulary words like "gratuitous," and "superfluous," that a Carlo education was not worth nearly so much of what relatively little my parents had.

I wanted to save them their money, but I couldn't leave Carlo. For my first few years, they would not entertain that possibility; they had dragged me to the entrance exam against my will for a reason. So instead of leaving the school and saving them a large sum of money, I saved them a little of it at a time and consistently skipped lunch—a meal that was one of Carlo's selling points.

Whereas students at other schools had no options for lunch unless they brought their options with them, at Carlo you could have angel food cake if you wanted, or perhaps chocolate pudding. You could have beans and rice or pork chops. You could pick and choose all of your lunch components; soup or corn, whatever. It was up to you, so long as they were serving it.

Other students relished this food, but I was too aware of how much it cost. At the end of the line sat one of the teachers, with a list of names and a calculator. He would count up the value of what was on each student's plate, and record it so that parents could be billed at the end of each month. Lunches routinely cost eight or ten dollars—an enormous sum, I thought. I refused to eat the stuff.

It helped that by the time I turned fourteen food did not appeal to me. Most of the time, I had no appetite at all; eating often made me feel vaguely nauseous, even when I was hungry. I also had a secret goal of weighing as little as possible—which must have had something to do with the nausea. I didn't know the first thing about physical exercise, and I certainly wasn't going to play any sports, so, as an alternative, for the first phase of my life at Carlo I chose to forego the midday meal and went hungry.

~

For a century and two years, starting in 1877, Carlo was a military school. By the turn of the 1980s, my mother explained to me more than once, the Vietnam War had rendered the armed forces unpopular, so Carlo went civilian. Evidence of its martial history remained, though. The football team was called the "Cadets." Hanging over the door to the canteen in the basement was a sign that read in metal letters, "Rifle Range."

The Aviator, an on-campus statue of a man in a flight suit, with wings, like an angel, was a monument to all the pilots who had attended Carlo and died in World War One. Situated in back of the main building, overlooking the dorms and teachers' houses below, he stood before a concrete balcony, looking pensive on a pedestal. The rest of campus lay beyond the aviator, all the way to the creek that marked its outer boundary. It was a common trick among the older, more athletic students to sprint across the green to the lookout behind the Aviator, level with his hat, then plant a foot on the balcony railing and leap with great agility over his head, to land on the grass more than a full story below.

Because Carlo had long since given up its affiliation with the armed forces, the uniform I wore to school in the mid-nineties was civilian. My parents purchased a blazer for me at the school canteen, and I had to wear it. It was navy blue and usually covered with dust, because someone sitting behind me in a class would brush his shoes against my blazer, and shoes at Carlo were unerringly dusty.

I had to wear a tie, but didn't know how to tie one. I didn't want to learn the technique, so instead I wore the same tie every day. My father established a knot on my behalf, before my first day in the seventh grade. After school, every day, for four years, I loosened it slightly to preserve the knot, only to tighten it again the next morning. The knot came out a handful of times in four years—an intermittent crisis—but otherwise it held in place.

If a student was a woman, she had to wear a grey or plaid skirt, a shirt with buttons down the front, and a fabric tie that buttoned under the neck.

These outfits and the young women who wore them were a sign of the times. Nine years after Carlo lost its military status, the school began admitting women, ending a restriction against them that had lasted more than a hundred years. I had no problem with this, but once, when I accompanied my mother after school to a local department store, an old woman pulled me aside as I stood in the checkout line in my uniform. She told me, without provocation, "Carlo has never been the same since they started letting girls in. It's been downhill ever since, just awful!"

Because of Carlo's fateful change in its policy toward women, my days there included Helen in them. A brunette of Polish descent, with pronounced lips and big, brown eyes, Helen was in nearly all of my classes in the ninth grade, and I found her distracting, as I wanted constantly to stare at her. I thought she was so beautiful that even when I was at home and couldn't see her, I still found her distracting. I couldn't get her out of my head; I thought about her all the time. I didn't try to date her, as I was too shy for actual romance. If I had ever so much as talked with Helen for more than a few minutes, I don't know what I would have said, so instead I looked at her, and thought about her, and probably made her think I was a strange person. My grades suffered, which, if she had known this, would have reinforced the opinion of the old lady at the checkout line.

Uniforms were to be bought at the school canteen, along with books and everything else. My mother must have spent a fortune there, on my behalf; countless times I stood by and watched as the attendant rang up the many purchases made on my behalf. In the four years I spent at Carlo my mother had to buy at least one blazer, one patch that was to be sewn onto the breast of the blazer, and one tie in the school's signature orange and black that was to be worn every Monday—but which I wore every day, since I didn't know how to tie the others. She bought pens, pencils, binders, notebooks, paper, textbooks, standard-ized gym outfits, expensive calculators the complexity and cost of which increased each year, protractors, graph paper—the list could go on. The supplies I had to own for attending Carlo must have cost ten times what I needed for a year at the public school. I thought of this constantly, as I skipped lunches and failed to perform well in every class that wasn't English or History.

One of the classes I did poorly in was eighth grade physical science, taught by the thickly bearded Mr. House, who has thankfully omitted himself from my bad dreams. Every year he traveled with a group of students to the Canadian wilderness, on a trip organized by the school, paid for by the parents. He was beloved for it, but I never joined him on those voyages, and so we never endeared ourselves to one another.

House gave his students a test, once, and on it was the ques-tion, "Could a paper clip ever be used as a tool for scientific measure-ment, and why?" Now that I am older and have taught at colleges for ten years, I understand that this was a vague and flawed question, but as a thirteen-year-old all I knew was that I didn't know the expected answer, so I wrote something I thought would sound good. To the whole class House read my wrong answer aloud, saying, "Listen to how one of you answered number five: 'Could a paper clip ever be used as a tool for scientific measurement, and why?' This guy wrote, 'Yes, because there are many objects used in a science lab setting, to accomplish different things, and that is one of the many objects that would fit in.'" Then he stared directly at me for a few very long seconds, before moving on to something else.

Mr. Miller taught Geometry to the eighth grade. Dr. Marks taught Biology to the ninth. Stalemated in a fierce conflict, Miller was a devout Christian, while Marks was an Atheist. Miller kept religious material posted on his classroom door, such as Christian-themed cartoons that weren't funny, and fliers for events held by the Fellowship of Christian Athletes. Marks had a PhD in entomology. His walls were covered with newspaper cartoons depicting evolution, and photos of Frank Zappa. Once, when Miller passed our classroom, Marks heard him walking through the hallway and interrupted himself to announce, loudly enough that Miller could hear, "Remember, the Bible is a book— it's a good book, but it's not the only book." Miller called to us from the hall, "No, it's *the* book." It must have bolstered the spirits of my pious classmates, but I, already a decided Atheist, sided with Marks. I still failed most of his tests.

Dr. Marks was the only teacher to address directly the problem of my grades. He pulled me aside one morning to ask, "What's wrong with you?" I had scored a forty percent on one of his tests. I told him I was having trouble studying, that I sat with my book and my notes for hours at a time, but couldn't retain a thing. I was telling him the truth, in the hallway outside his classroom. I didn't know what to do.

I was not telling him the full truth, though, much as I, to my surprise, wanted to. For a moment I considered letting him in on my secret: I had just recently grown infatuated with Helen. My devotion from afar, to the person I imagined she might be, had helped reduce my grades from middling to abysmal. I wanted to tell him this, but didn't.

I could be counted on to think about or stare at Helen more or less every moment of each day, and the things that distracted me from her were notable. One was *The Hitchhiker's Guide to the Galaxy*, a copy of which I carried for the many weeks it took me to read it, catching a few paragraphs at a time between classes. Another distraction was a snake attack.

Among the fixtures of Dr. Marks's biology classroom were the corpse of a tarantula that hung from the ceiling, a model of the human skull, and a live Burmese Python named Rasta. I can't remember its exact length; I seem to recall it being twelve feet, but I suspect it must have been more like eight. Either way, Rasta was gigantic, especially to a fifteen-year-old, and she spent most of her time in a tank in the corner, brooding thick and languid, protected from the students by a pane of glass. Marks, an expert on snakes, would let Rasta out on occasion, so that she could slink lazily through the room, making half the students nervous, but thrilling the other half, as Rasta was far more interesting than anything else at Carlo, including my grandfather's cannon. I once watched as Rasta splayed herself across the classroom entrance and defecated for a full minute, lurching toward the window and leaving in her wake what resembled a long pound of meat loaf. During the occasional class, Marks would feed Rasta, depositing a large rat in her tank so that students could watch her feast.

I never had a chance to watch Rasta eat a small mammal, but I came close to seeing her eat a large one. One morning Erin, another ninth grader whose biology class met later in the day, brought a chicken from her farm, so that Marks could feed it to his snake in the afternoon. She and the rest of her class would watch, and we of the morning class were jealous and embittered that we would not witness the scene.

The chicken arrived in a Styrofoam cooler, with a brick lain on top to prevent its escape. Marks placed it under Rasta's tank, which stood on legs a few feet high in a corner of the room. I sat next to it, three seats back. In the front row, beside the tank's glass door, sat Grant, a lanky classmate with massive glasses and a blond bowl cut. Marks opened the tank to let Rasta roam, but for thirty minutes she didn't venture out. Instead she loomed on the edge, bunched up near her open door.

Marks was lecturing. I wasn't paying attention; I was trying to sneak glances at Helen, who sat clear across the room. But for a few moments, something happened that I considered more interesting than Helen. Fast enough than I could hardly see it take place—so fast that a moment passed before I recognized what it was that had attached itself to Grant and was wrapping itself around his arm—Rasta struck. One moment she was lolling on the edge of her tank, the next her teeth were dug into Grant's ribcage, under his left arm. Her mouth was open wide, her jaws splayed against his white dress shirt, part of it turning red.

Grant turned as white as his shirt's unbloody parts and pleaded, "Oh god, get it off me." His cry for help given, he fell off his chair, arms held out before him, as Marks, without hesitation, leapt over his desk and pounced on Rasta, prying her mouth open with his hands, her teeth cutting his fingers.

In what must have been less than a minute, Rasta was dislodged. By then, I and my classmates had plastered ourselves to the wall on the opposite side of the room. Marks took Grant into the hallway, leaving the thirty of us with Rasta, who had crept under her tank to sulk. Like we would in a fire drill, I and the others filed out, hugging the walls. As one of the Wallace twins passed by, Rasta lashed out one more time from under the tank, but smacked her face against the Plexiglas door that hung in her way.

Twenty minutes later, it seemed that everyone in the school knew about the snake attack. I felt like a celebrity, as I had been within the length of a Burmese Python of the incident." I got to tell a half-dozen eager listeners about it, before it became old news. The scene had effectively broken the tedium of Carlo for a full day, after which point the tedium returned and I went back to feeling like myself, perpetually unbrushed hair included. Rasta was soon gone; Marks had to sell her, along with most of the snakes he kept in his house on campus. I resumed thinking about Helen, and continued to do so for another year.

~

Perhaps I have such bad dreams about Carlo because of the lighting. All of the lights there were fluorescent, like a department store, which was the first mistake, but even for fluorescent lights their illumination was pitiful. The hallway lights were so dim that in order to see past lockers and other students, between classes, I had to squint. I heard from someone, I can't recall whom, that the school was inspected every five years or so, and that when an inspector came periodically the headmaster turned up the lights to a more humane level, then dimmed them again as soon as he left, to save money on electricity.

Others overlooked the lighting problem in favor of Carlo's other flaws. Many of my peers despised the headmaster. This was predictable enough, given the general opinion of figureheads among the

34

adolescents who are subject to them. Their reason was that he harmed them physically. At lunch, the graying Italian-American man would seek out a row of boys and grip the nearest one by the neck and squeeze, then stop at the next and throttle him by the arm, then give the next a hard pinch on the ear, and so on. This never bothered me. It was what I recognized as tough love, and I had experienced it firsthand for years from my three elder brothers. When other students complained about the mild abuse, though, I told them I agreed it was inappropriate, for empathy's sake.

~

One morning, before school, in the ninth grade, I ate five bowls of Fruity Pebbles, a breakfast cereal I liked. I had them with milk, one after another, and told my mother I might be starting a growth spurt, as a feast like that was uncommon for me; I usually went without breakfast. All day I tasted in back of my throat the sugar and artificial flavors I had shoveled into myself. At lunch, I wasn't hungry. Then, in the library during study hall, in the seventh period of the day—next to last—I got up and rushed to the men's room. I knew what was coming, from the tightness in my throat and my watering eyes.

I burst into a stall, just in time, and in a torrent vomited all five bowls of milk and Fruity Pebbles. Some made it to the toilet, but most spilled all over the floor.

Whenever I throw up, to this day, I scream involuntarily. Of all the things I do it is the strangest. My voice erupts from my throat, along with whatever I have eaten, through the retching and reversed digestion. Vomiting, for me, is an excruciating affair, in part because of the heaving stomach acid, but also because of this additional strain on my voice.

Some react to my vomit noise by laughing. Others back away. Court Meadows, in the stall next to mine, responded by asking through the partition, "Do you need me to get a janitor?"

I told him no. It was my mess. I hacked up what was left of my breakfast as Court fled the room. Then I went to work.

The stall was a catastrophe. Even after I flushed the toilet, the site was covered with purple slime. I spent the next fifteen minutes of increasing nausea mopping by hand the mess I had made.

I flushed the newly immaculate toilet, but the wad of paper towels—not designed for being flushed—caught in the drain and refused to go any further. There was no plunger. I reached my hand through the pool of water and pulled out the towels, then flushed them again.

When I returned to the school library, I told my friends about this episode proudly, as if I had accomplished something, which was not how I behaved when tests I'd nearly failed were returned to me, and when I neglected to turn in Latin translations because they took too long and I lost interest in them.

~

Halfway through the ninth grade, I started doing all of my schoolwork in my parents' basement. This is more significant than it may sound. Attending Carlo meant spending six or seven hours (not an exaggeration) on homework every day, so to do all of my work in the basement meant that I spent half of every waking day underground. There was a furnace down there, a concrete floor, and a lot of unused furniture. I found a table and chair and swept them off. There I spent most of my time, out of sight of my parents and siblings, blissfully alone. I had almost no interest in this work, but I liked to be by myself.

Most of what I did in the basement for Carlo is lost to memory, but one project I will never forget. In the tenth grade I was ordered to write a biography paper, on a person of my choice. I had written one on George Orwell in the eighth grade, but I didn't know where to turn next. I was in the kitchen, complaining to my parents that I had no ideas—I think my father suggested Ronald Reagan—when my elder brother David overheard me from the dining room. He came in and ordered me to "Do Frank Zappa." He had never shown much interest in me; he is nearly ten years older than I, and had always been a distant presence in my life. On this point, though, he was insistent.

I was so taken aback by David's enthusiasm that when he said "Do Frank Zappa" again I agreed to his suggestion. A few days later he brought me a brown paper bag filled with research materials: forty Zappa albums, six books on him, and the film 200 Motels.

The paper I wrote was a mess, as I was overwhelmed, and I was fourteen, but I learned an awful lot about Frank Zappa, more than I ever thought I would know. I listened to all of the albums I had time to hear. I read, here and there, from the books. I contemplated the Zombie-Woof. I got an A.

Monstrous French poodles and saintly pancake breakfasts included, Zappa's rhetoric made a strong impression on me, largely because he criticized so many things that were taken for granted in my world. These included America's education system, and basic teenage rituals, like dating, but also organized religion and drug abuse. I had disdained religion, dating, and drugs—inarticulately—but now I had heard someone voice the things I felt, and do it with guitar solos.

I had suspected for years that attendance at Carlo was not worth its price, but had never done anything about it. It wasn't until soon after I wrote my Frank Zappa paper that I felt I should do something about it. When I told my parents Carlo wasn't working for me, I felt like I knew what I was talking about. I went to them one evening, after some hours spent, like so many others, reading beneath their feet, and said I'd like to leave Carlo and attend the public school. They, to my surprise, acquiesced readily.

By the tenth grade, students in my class at Carlo were dropping out like flies, consigning themselves to education by the state, and thereby saving their parents many thousands of dollars. I wondered if the men who ran the school were getting desperate, when I heard that the administrator Mr. Sherman told my departing classmate Mike, as he cleaned out his locker, that he would never make it to college if he went to a public school.

Many students at Carlo were terrified of the public high school, and of the students they imagined were enrolled there. "People will beat you up, every day, if you go," my classmates would say, and they meant it. They thought anyone who defected would surely die. Nearly all of Carlo's students believed in the terminal fate that awaited them at Park, in case they did something to warrant expulsion, or in case their parents could not afford the next year's tuition. Most of them were wealthy and docile enough to never have to worry about these events, but rumors and fears persisted.

I was surprised to find, when I first entered Wheeling Park, that no one could tell I had just transferred from Carlo. In fact, the only people who noticed me at all were the friends I had already made outside of school.

~

If my parents had never sent me to Carlo, they would have saved themselves nearly thirty thousand dollars. They could use it, today. They could, for that matter, have put the money aside and waited until next week to surprise me with it, as a gift. I would be overjoyed to receive it. I would travel to another country.

I have not returned to Carlo's campus in many years, but I am reminded of it when I dream and every time I go home to see my parents, because they still live half a mile from its main building, and it comes up in conversation between my siblings—some of whom continue to resent the teachers whose pedagogies they endured there, some of whom continue to admire them.

At twenty-seven, on an afternoon in Missouri—500 miles from my home town—I met a college professor who turned out to have once known my elder brother David, because she had long ago attended Carlo, and David and her brother had been close friends, at Carlo. Her last year attending the school was my first year there, which meant that we must have crossed each other's paths, as so few students attend there at one time. We must have met each other, silently, in a hallway far away, and now here we were, talking about our lives at Carlo.

In my waking life as well as in my dreams, despite my physical remoteness from Carlo, which has only increased with time, I have had a hard time getting away from it. I expect I always will. If I learned nothing else there, I understand that to spend mornings and afternoons in a place for four years entails merging that place with the person you are, or strive to be, whether you like it or not.

DIRTY LAUNDRY

I returned to my apartment in Athens, Ohio, at the end of a summer spent elsewhere, to find in my closet someone's dirty laundry. In a black garbage bag were two pairs of panties, a bra, a tank top, some shirts, a black skirt, and a pair of long socks.

Sarah, a young woman from Leipzig, had subleased the one-bedroom unit in my absence. She had moved out the day before I returned. She must have put the clothes in the closet and forgotten them, I thought; they certainly weren't left there for me. We had not been lovers, or friends. We had barely ever spoken—never about our personal lives, nor about our underwear—but now, unlikely as it seemed, I was in possession of her underwear. I could do whatever I wanted with them. I could wear them or sell them, and she wouldn't know.

Rather than do these things, at least at first, I left the clothes as they were and wrote about them in my diary. I wrote, "It's almost as though she's still here. Something of her still hangs in the air, the air she breathed in July. It will haunt me until the day I leave, and I cannot take these clothes with me when I move out." I was right about the last part. I would have to do something with Sarah's clothes, but in part because I had never owned women's clothing, I didn't know what to do with them.

I knew I could throw the clothes away, but effort and money had been spent to create and then acquire them, so I felt it would have been wasteful to consign them to a landfill. I asked my women friends—I knew no drag queens—if they might like a free skirt or shirt. No one wanted them, though, or they doubted Sarah's clothes would fit, so the bag remained where Sarah had left it, most of the time.

A month after I found Sarah's long, discarded socks among her other things, I put them on. I didn't think the socks would be sexually arousing to wear, or emotionally fulfilling, but I had never worn such lengthy socks and I was curious to know what I'd been missing for 23 years. They were thick and made of a fabric I couldn't name. They were the first women's clothes to ever interest me without at the time being worn or taken off by a woman.

They fit well and reached higher than my knees, but they didn't belong on my feet. Their off-white color didn't suit my skin tone—and it felt, as I pulled each one over an ankle, like I was doing something wrong, and not only because I had always worn shorter socks. My interest in Sarah's clothes had gone too far. It was as though when I adorned myself with the forfeited garments I had on vestigial pieces of Sarah, as if she should feel me wearing her socks. I took them off. I kept my distance from the bag in the closet, but I talked about its contents with my friends.

Most people, when I told them about Sarah's abandoned laundry, were less interested in it than they were in other things, like movies and their own lives. A friend suggested I throw the clothes away—which would have been expedited by the fact that when I found them they were in a garbage bag. I wondered if Sarah had meant to throw the clothes out but had forgotten to, in which case she would be upset to learn that I hadn't done it for her, and was instead telling friends about her clothes, even if I omitted their more sultry details for decorum's sake.

When I told my friend Paul about the clothes at lunch, he asked why I hadn't washed them and said it was the first thing he would have done. I admitted, puzzled, that it hadn't occurred to me. At the time I couldn't figure out why not, but now, years later, I understand that Paul thought of this because he owned a house with a washer and dryer. I didn't have ready access to such appliances, so to wash Sarah's laundry would have meant a long walk to a Laundromat and at least an hour devoted to cleaning things whose owner would never see them again.

When she departed Athens for Germany, Sarah may have forgotten altogether the castoffs in my closet that made up a fraction of the world's evidence of her passage through it. Having left America, she had other things—German things—to think about. Still, at night, alone, in Ohio, despite the Ohio things that worried me, I often lay awake with my mind fixed on the undone laundry.

~

The apartment I rented was on the second floor of a building that stood on the slope of an Appalachian hill, on a street occupied mostly by college students. It consisted of a bedroom, a living room, a kitchenette and a bathroom, all of which were old enough to have started disintegrating. The carpet was torn under the doorframes, the ceiling panels water-stained.

When I returned from my summer away, even before I saw the bag of laundry, it was clear that Sarah had left an impression on my home and that she knew more than I did about interior decorating. She had rearranged the living room to make more space for her, and me, to walk through. With a blanket she had covered the loveseat my brother had given me, which was stricken with permanent, multicolored stains left by his two sons. She had transformed the unsightly piece of upholstered furniture into something that was inoffensive—unless I lifted the blanket and peered underneath. In this way Sarah was a blessing, like Casper the Friendly Ghost.

From what I could tell, from the ways she had improved my home, and from the bottle I found in the bathroom that contained a substance that would stave off mold if I sprayed it into the shower after each use, Sarah was better at living in my home than I was. Most of the bottles I bought and emptied there contained Miller High Life, and they did nothing to prevent the onset of mold.

I had, on moving into it, named my apartment The Honeydew Melon. The name was a joke, at first, something to enter as the first line of my address so that it appeared on junk mail. But naming the place had an effect, like naming a dog; it made the space I lived in more familiar. It might have also been a form of mail fraud, but I soon discovered that the name served another purpose still. It provided me a way to claim the space I took up, with my body, sheets, and predominantly brown wardrobe, to make it feel like my own, though I merely rented it. Sarah had made my home more handsome, and cleaner, but she had also made the Melon seem less mine than hers. When I returned to it, for a moment I didn't recognize the place. Sarah was like a squatter who, by inhabiting and improving an abandoned building, earns the right to live there and renders immaterial its previous owner.

~

In the months I spent living with Sarah's laundry, I wondered if I, too, had ever abandoned things when moving out of previous apartments.

I remembered, soon after I first wondered this, that I most certainly had. When I departed the first apartment I ever lived in, my friends and I left a menagerie of insect corpses smeared on our walls. We had spent our two years there killing moths, spiders, and other such creatures when they entered our home. Rather than clean them we would label each one with the time and date of its murder. When we moved out, we removed the post-it notes that served as markers but left the bugs, because we knew our landlord had no intention of returning our security deposit.

In the second apartment I ever inhabited, I got into an argument with my girlfriend, an angry drunk who was, on one particular night, drunk. Her temper erupted and she threw at me a copy of *Catch-22* after trying in vain to tear it in half. She snatched from my desk a glass full of water and lobbed it at the nearest wall. It broke, soaking the floor and littering it with tiny pieces of glass that remained at least as long as my lease kept me in residence, despite my repeated efforts to vacuum them up. I would catch sight of the tiny shards as they glittered at me stubbornly from the carpet, and I wonder if they do it still, for someone else's eyes.

For as long as I lived in the Honeydew Melon, pasted in odd, unlikely corners were stickers the size of quarters with faded images on them of flower arrangements. One was on the door to my living room, one on a windowpane, one on the ceiling. Yet another was upside down on the wall inside my closet, placed so that someone would have to snoop around for traces of other people to find it. I hadn't put them up. They could have been there for a decade. I never removed them. They served as evidence that the Melon had accumulated remnants of strangers long before Sarah, or I, came and went.

I considered it inevitable that when I moved I would leave something in the Melon by mistake—a paper clip, breadcrumbs, or dead skin and discarded eyelashes. My landlord had made no apparent effort to clean the apartment before I moved in and must have neglected to do it when I left. The Melon, dutiful as always, would take possession of what remained—the next resident's inheritance—as soon as I was gone. It had done as much for Sarah, and for the legion of strangers who had lived between its walls, eating, sleeping, and being kept up at night by the neighbors.

~

My neighbors were by far the loudest people I had ever been kept awake by. One night per week, the man across the hall would stay up late, drinking with his friends and playing video games. On one inspired night, he and they chanted, stomped against the floor, and pounded the walls, one of them giving off a prolonged shriek every few minutes until 5:00 in the morning. It sounded like they were having a violent, celebratory orgy.

The apartment above mine was inhabited by a rotation of loud people. The first was a man who would play, through his stereo, hours of bass-heavy music at high volume, all night. He accosted me one morning on my way out of the building to ask if I had called the police to report a noise violation. Someone had done this, he said, his eyes burning. It had been me, but when I lied and denied the charge, he proceeded to tell me a story: he used to live in the country and kept many dogs in his yard, but one day he enraged a man who later came to his yard and shot to death all but one of his dogs.

Eventually, he was replaced by a young college student, a woman with an unfortunate boyfriend. One night they fought and she threw him out, howling and slamming the door, demanding that he never return. Later that night he returned, scratching at her door, which was adjacent to mine. As he cooed to her, begging to be let in, she sat on

43

the other side of her door and wept. I sat at my desk, listening with my head in my hands and wondered how many bad scenes the walls would contain before they finally came to pieces.

~

When summer returned, I had to move away, and Sarah's clothes had to be reckoned with. Taking them with me would have meant claiming them as my property, but I didn't want to encumber myself with things I should never have had in the first place, so I made an active effort to dispose of the heavy garbage bag. I showed it to my friend Melanie and asked if she wanted anything in it. She remarked that she clearly didn't share Sarah's figure. She tried on the skirt, but it didn't fit, and then carried off a shirt anyway.

I didn't mention it, but when Melanie took the shirt I regretted ever bringing the clothes to her attention. It felt like she had taken something of mine.

Soon, Melanie found a woman in need of a skirt. As soon as we were introduced, this woman asked if she could have Sarah's. This skirtless woman was, like Sarah, a visiting student from Leipzig, and I saw that to hand the skirt over would have meant sending it on a trajectory back in Sarah's direction, but instead I told her I didn't have the skirt anymore. I told her I had already given the clothes away.

The day my lease ended, I was glad to leave the Melon. The woman upstairs had procured a little dog. When she wasn't home, which was most of the time, it pressed its nose against the screen of her open window and barked at nothing in particular. I could hear it for hours at a time, every single day.

The last thing I removed from the Melon was Sarah's dirty laundry. Nine months after her return to Germany, I rummaged through the sack she'd left and tossed her underwear into my last trash bag, as I thought she might have liked me to have done long before. The rest I carried to a Salvation Army donation bin, half a mile away.

More than I cared what became of my Fiestaware, more than I cared about the Melon itself, with its ancient carpet and walls I had painted green, I cared about Sarah's bag of dirty laundry. I worried what might happen to the clothes when they left my custody. I knew, as I

44

walked the bag down to the Salvation Army's roadside metal box, that I was letting go of something important. In an apartment full of objects—kitchen table, hand blender, dull chef's knife, unused knife sharpener, lamp—Sarah's sack of clothing was a thing—or thing filled with things—that seemed to mean something.

Standing before the donation bin, I thought I might actually miss it, this sack of someone else's stuff that had occupied my idle thoughts for nearly a year. I felt as though by having shared the Honeydew Melon, by having been so close for so much of the time, it and I had bonded. I pushed the metal door open and dropped the bag inside. As far as I know, I never saw its contents again.

PIGS AND EGGPLANTS

My friend Erich cooked a steak one night, years ago, and threw it in a blender with beer, a dollar bill, and A-1 sauce. He took up a collection, and promised his best friend Jerry ten dollars, plus what we'd collected, if he swallowed the liquid result through a funnel. Jerry took the money, and drank the steak. Then he guzzled two bottles of Worcestershire sauce for free, and threw up in Erich's alley.

I used to eat meat, too. Later that very summer, in fact, my best friend Charlie's neighbors had a block party. Homeowners grilled ribs, chicken breasts, steaks and slabs of pork. They drank beer. They talked about football, ate what they could, and stuffed what was left into a cooler. Charlie and I arrived late with our good friend Rob from another part of town. The three of us joined a mid-street circle of drunk people and failed to fit in.

The party broke up halfway through our second drinks. Women stumbled up the street as their kids went whirring past them. One man compelled the stragglers to go home by playing some Pink Floyd album that came from deep space. Before long, even he was gone. Charlie, Rob and I had the street to ourselves.

We discovered the meat in the cooler. I had never seen so many warm carcasses together in one box. We found some other coolers, filled with the kind of beer we could not afford. It oozed through us, thick and expensive, like dollars and meat pureed in a blender. We gorged ourselves until daylight shone over the hills, until my torso was bursting with animals. Then I swilled beer until I nearly vomited, waited for space to free up, chewed the flesh off another fat rib, and swallowed. Charlie and Rob did the same. We must have consumed several whole creatures between us, laughing with disbelief.

I would never have done this, I now realize, with onions and yellow squash. If I tried to eat as much bread as I did meat that night, I would not get far into the bread.

I was not yet a vegetarian when I had lunch at a Washington, D.C. steakhouse one July afternoon, with some petroleum lobbyists. Because I still ate meat, I ordered a chicken sandwich. A white-haired millionaire beside me asked accusingly, "Do you have something against steak? Why wouldn't you want to eat steak?"

He was angry. My aunt, who had brought me there, looked on, confused.

The millionaire got incredulous with me once more during the meal, when he asked if I would accept a free Volkswagen bug, if one were offered to me as a gift. I told him I would. I didn't own a car, and could have used a Volkswagen bug.

He looked hurt. He let the subject go. He scarfed down the dead mammal on his plate while I picked at the flightless bird in front of me.

Before I discovered vegetables for all that they can be, food was uncomplicated fuel. I ate it so that I would no longer be hungry, and could then devote myself to other things. I survived on cream of chicken, mostly, and spent the last year of college severely constipated, perplexed as to why that was, even as I ate. Eventually, my then-girlfriend Valerie convinced me to see a doctor, who took an x-ray of my bowels and said he could hardly believe that so much food could have lodged itself in a man of my size.

For a week, I supplemented my diet with milk of magnesia. Otherwise, I did not change a thing.

The following summer, I worked at a remote candy store, and after six weeks I developed a severe, incessant pain in my abdomen. I would sprawl on a bed each day, stomach throbbing, until I felt well enough to eat more chicken from a can and then go to work. This pain was higher up and sharper than the previous one in my guts. Valerie drove me to the nearest hospital, where a nurse attempted to discover the cause of this agony through a fruitless ultrasound test. On the way back, disappointed and still in pain, it hit me. "Oh," I said and wondered aloud if my stomach hurt so much, maybe, because I'd been eating milkshakes and candy all summer, eight hours at a time.

It was a relief, to think of this, but ever since then I have missed the chocolate covered cashews, the tiramisu, the jellybeans, and the reeling dizziness from all this stuff I consumed incrementally in the candy shop's storage room.

My conversion to vegetarianism prompted me to slow down and pay attention to food. Soon I could even cook, a little, and when I sweat I smell a little like a plant.

I never pushed my eating habits on others, but then when I caught my girlfriend Aurora cutting up raw pork I told her, "That pig ate a kitten. If you eat it, you're basically eating a kitten."

She ate the kitten. I filled myself with potatoes, and watched.

In high school I used to sit in my political science class, bored, and trace the veins on my arm, or knead my calf to find where shin met muscle. I was often thinking that if someone ate me I would taste pretty good. I imagined severing my left forearm—which I rarely used—and frying it for lunch. My friends could have had a barbecue. I could have joined them, in some capacity. I was glad to graduate from high school and move on to other things.

After I watched Aurora eat the kitten, these thoughts returned. In a dream, I chewed two fingers off my left hand. They tasted bitter, and I regretted at once my decision to eat them. I had not even been hungry.

If I were filled with seeds, or if my flesh had the texture of eggplant, I would never touch another vegetable. If I were green and partly translucent, I would let celery be rather than devour it with peanut butter. I became a vegetarian because it felt natural. I will stay a vegetarian because when strangers eat prime rib it looks like they are chewing and swallowing my friend Eli, whom I have not seen in years.

I went to New Orleans with Aurora. A couple of curious tourists, at an upstairs restaurant which teetered over a bar on the first floor, we ordered frogs' legs. I eat fish, because this adheres to the rule of consuming only what I do not resemble when I have my clothes and skin off. I decided that frogs are equivalent to fish, because fish and amphibians alike dwell in water, have funny eyes, and look confused. The legs were delicious, somewhere in texture between crab and octopus.

Aurora ate one leg and stopped. She told me she could not continue, because the amphibian limbs resembled human legs, miniaturized. She said that, ever since she ate the kitten, meat products had appealed to her less and less. "You keep showing me the parts of your arm that would taste good," she added. "And it grosses me out." This was not my intention, but I knew that her diet had been changing. The day prior, she'd ordered a meat muffaletta and not eaten it, because it turned out to be a wanton pile of lunchmeat on bread, and this bothered her. I, meanwhile, chomped my different muffaletta—a mound of olives on bread—and watched her, wondering what the problem was.

Aurora had been a vegetarian for years. When she was eleven, she consumed eight eggs in one sitting. I have yet to demonstrate such extreme dedication to not consuming fully grown animals, so I was impressed when I learned this biographical detail. I felt like I was dating Cool Hand Luke.

A meatless dietary tendency was creeping up on Aurora once again. I was helping.

One night we watched the film *Babe*. During the scene when Farmer Hoggett and his wife eat a Christmas duck, and Ferdinand the duck looks on in despair because his friend is dead on a serving plate, Aurora said, "This movie was made by vegetarians." She sounded distressed, not unlike Ferdinand the duck.

We watched the Wallace and Gromit film *Curse of the Were-Rabbit*, in which people appear to eat only vegetables, and a rabbit is, through science, endowed with speech and a passion for cheese. He wears a green shirt, like Wallace the clay person does. As the credits rolled, I had to wonder if there is indeed a vegetarian propaganda effort at work, which aims to make children eat plants. If so, it doesn't bother me. At least Babe does not try to sell them cigarettes.

Aurora and I were not children, but we did watch their movies. I took her to see *The Proposition*, because we were adults, but she couldn't stomach it. She left just as a minor character was having his throat stomped until he died. Aurora had lasted through the scene wherein a man is speared and vomits blood, but this was too much. It did not compel her to eat more vegetables, but it did make her wary of letting me decide what movies we watch in dark theaters together.

Someone once said to me, "Listen. There's a reason we have these sharp teeth, and they're for tearing meat apart, and that's all." Meanwhile I have lots of incisors, but I don't wake each morning with a powerful craving for elk shoulders. My sharp teeth work beautifully for shredding eggplant.

The enamel blades that line the average jaw must have been indispensable before early humans learned to cook eggplant, and when, hunched in their caves, they ate things that were not marshmallows. Despite my fangs, I love to eat oranges, broccoli, peaches, noodles, and granola, none of which come from dead animals.

Yogurt makes me feel good. I used to eat it every morning, before I ventured out among the barbarians. To this day, I visit food courts and cafeterias where they chew and swallow food that once could scream and snuggle. At night I dream of avocadoes.

GUTS

I was twenty-two when I ate my last hamburger. My mother cooked it. Halfway through the sandwich, I took a large bite, and by surprise the wet bun and wet meat turned my stomach. I coaxed the mouthful down my throat slowly, gagging at the nearest plate. It digested without further incident, but I knew I would never swallow another speck of dead cow. A year later, on a hillside, at a picnic, I had my last serving of chicken legs. When the feast ended, I saw the freshly stripped bones on my plate, and my greasy fingers, and thought what I had done had not been worth it; I hadn't even enjoyed the deep-fried yield of several creatures' slaughter. Since then I have refused to eat animals, so I touch them only when I pet cats and dogs.

Many good people have chosen meatless diets. Leonardo da Vinci did it. So did Kafka, Tolstoy, and Emerson. Prince didn't eat meat, and neither did Michel de Montaigne. Neither did Thomas Paine, though my mother told me, in a recent e-mail, that he was a "rascal."

Despite my passion for eggplants, and my years as a vegetarian, I have never deterred someone else from eating meat. I have not tried. I would like to see people eat more vegetables and less meat—if not swear it off altogether—but rather than tell them this I leave them alone. Most

53

people, I assume, don't want to hear that vegetables might be better for them than steaks, that modern methods of handling livestock are cruel. They want to get on with their lives, chicken soups and ham sandwiches. It is not my place to stop them.

Adolf Hitler, an ardent vegetarian, would disagree. According to food writer Bee Wilson, he was as vocal about vegetables as he was about other things. When meat-eaters joined him at meals, "He would harangue them for hypocrisy," for eating creatures they would lack the nerve to slaughter. He once said, "'That shows how cowardly people are [...] They can't face doing certain horrible things themselves, but they enjoy the benefits without a pang of conscience.'"

After one meeting with Hitler, Joseph Goebbels wrote in a private diary that his boss "believes more than ever that meat-eating is harmful to humanity. Of course he knows that during the war we cannot completely upset our food system. After the war, however, he intends to tackle this problem also. Maybe he is right. Certainly the arguments that he adduces in favor of his standpoint are very compelling."

This is the rub—or one of them—of Hitler's eating habits: I am at a loss for how to make them appealing to others, and he was not. He extolled the meatless diet. He argued for it so fervently that a seasoned propagandist could not help but praise it in writing.

Another rub is that if we take Goebbels at his word—which is, admittedly, hazardous, considering his role as propaganda minister—Hitler considered meat consumption a "problem" among other problems, which included the presence of Jews in Europe, and the existence of Communists and others still. But these "problems," and their solutions which exceeded atrocity, took precedence over the issue of meat consumption in the Third Reich, the halting of which, while controversial, should not have caused the mass murder of its people.

Not only was Hitler a charismatic vegetarian—at least among Nazis—he was supposedly thorough about it. He teased Eva Braun for wearing makeup, because of the animals killed for its production.

It has been speculated that Hitler's diet had something to do with the suicide of his niece, Geli Raubal. In 1931, she was found in her bedroom, in his apartment, with a hole in her lung, made with his gun. It was said that Hitler refused to let her see her fiancé in Vienna, that

Hitler controlled her obsessively, and that her death followed a violent quarrel with him. Some claim that Raubal's death made a vegetarian of Hitler, that after it a disgust with meat overtook him, suddenly and for good.

Scholars see in Hitler's rejection of meat the influence of composer Richard Wagner. A series of his essays from the 1870s argue that centuries of interbreeding had mixed Aryan with Jewish blood, and that one means for reversing this contamination was to make the Aryans vegetarians. Wagner's is a logic I would avoid, if I tried to convince others to stop eating meat, but it must have made sense to Hitler.

Hitler himself maintained that his evasion of meat was practical. He said, "As long as I ate meat, I would sweat profusely at rallies. I would drink four pints of beer and lose nine pounds. When I became a vegetarian, I just needed a sip of water every now and then."

Hitler's Table Talk, a meticulous transcript of statements Hitler made at meals, is, in the words of Hannah Arendt, "a peculiar book," in which Hitler mostly speaks to military advisors, and often talks vegetables. In December 1941, Hitler spoke for the children, saying, "If I offer a child the choice between a pear and a piece of meat, he'll quickly choose the pear. That's his atavistic instinct speaking." At lunch in the Reich Chancellery, on April 25, 1942, Hitler said, "the dog, which is carnivorous, cannot compare in performance with the horse, which is vegetarian." Later that year, on the 8th of July, at dinner, Hitler told Wilhelm Keitel that his sheepdog Blondi was nearly vegetarian herself. He once concluded a dinner monologue by announcing, "There's one thing I can predict to eaters of meat, that the world of the future will be vegetarian!"

Never do I speak of lettuce and carrots with such certainty. I lack a dangerous charisma like Hitler's, as well as his oratory skills, and I cannot present my food preference as something crucial that should be written in private diaries. I am far too timid to rhetorically trample the diets of others, or even to prod eaters of meat to question what appears on their plates. I am interested in food, and must eat it several times a day, but I am not openly passionate about it.

I am also staunchly opposed to the use of torture, the overuse of cars, and the failure of some of my closest friends to vote or read newspapers. But I never so much as mention these problems to them.

I keep my mouth shut, mostly out of politeness, and I wonder just how wrong and backward is this failure to voice my convictions.

I haven't spent much time reading *Hitler's Table Talk*, as I would rather read authors who are not responsible for the Holocaust. But I am struck, when perusing transcripts of conversations had in Hitler's dining room, by how seldom those who are not Hitler make themselves heard. In Arendt's words, "his partners at table would, it seems, swallow just about anything." There are interjections, most of them affirmative, from Martin Bormann and others. They speak, but no one seems to question Hitler, even when what he says is absurd. If I were to say tomorrow, at lunch with my wife, "when I meet children, I think of them as if they were my own. They all belong to me," she would at least object, if not send me away, but when Hitler said it, in July 1941, his talk pushed ever forward, unhindered by the sycophants surrounding him.

I like to think that I would not restrain myself in the presence of a megalomaniac, that if I could have had dinner with the Inner Circle I would have voiced my protest against the madness at the tyrant's table. But I worry that this probably isn't true. If only out of politeness, not to mention fear, I would likely have sat quietly, and maybe, at most, have traded knowing glances with Albert Speer, when Hitler said something especially out of line. I would keep my thoughts to myself.

~

In 1943, Hitler suffered from indigestion, so he hired Marlene von Exner, a twenty-four-year-old dietician from Vienna, to be his personal cook. Traudl Junge, Hitler's secretary, describes von Exner in a postwar memoir as "Dark haired, well built, full of the vivacious charm of Vienna, frank and amusing." She had previously cooked for Ion Antonescu, the Romanian dictator whose reign caused the deaths of roughly 400,000 people. By preparing him lobster, caviar, and a multitude of elaborate dishes, she had remedied his ailing stomach. When Hitler heard of this success, he offered her a job, and she accepted with reluctance.

Von Exner deplored Hitler's vegetarian diet. Junge writes, he "wanted nothing but his one-pot dishes, carrots with potatoes, and boring soft-boiled eggs." Von Exner "wailed, 'He'll never thrive on food like this.'"

Hitler, fond of hearing tales of von Exner's family life in Vienna, liked her. When Antonescu sent her a spontaneous present, a fox terrier puppy, Hitler grew indignant and said, "'What a Balkan like Antonescu can do, I can do better.'" He ordered Bormann to find a better dog, and the Reichsleiter procured for the chef a prize-winning, pedigree fox terrier.

Von Exner, responsible for two dogs she had no time for, "tearing her hair out" in exasperation at this unwanted attention, began sneaking marrowbone broth into Hitler's vegetable soups. He supposedly loved the new turn his food had taken, the way it tasted suddenly, richly different, but he didn't know its cause. He was eating liquid meat, and no one said a word.

At least one author celebrates this triumph over Hitler. I am reluctant to join her. There is a kind of justice in violating the dietary preference of a man who committed crimes on a vastly more awful scale, but at the same time, it seems a feeble gesture, to gloat over a thwarted vegetarian, no matter who he is. There are better ways to resist a Fascist, and I have other reasons to admire von Exner.

According to Junge, von Exner's resistance was not confined to the silent and culinary. When they ate together, which they did often, she stood up to Hitler. She upbraided him, saying, "'My Fuhrer, you promised to give Vienna, the pearl of Austria, a golden setting. But your people are destroying more of the old culture of Vienna than they build up.'"

Junge fails to note whether von Exner protested other things, if perhaps she went so far as to criticize the Final Solution. She was once an enthusiastic Nazi, but when "Nazi government and the war came to Austria" her fervency waned. I wonder what the cook said at dinner that escaped transcription.

Junge writes that von Exner "smoked like a chimney;" and that she assured her "she would be Hitler's cook only until he found a cigarette end in his cocoa." Eventually someone did—more or less—and discovered that von Exner's great-grandmother was Jewish. It meant catastrophe for her, naturally, as she worked for Nazis. Her engagement to an SS officer, which had taken place despite her hatred for the SS, was called off. Promising to Aryanize her family as consolation, Hitler fired her and sent her back to Vienna, where, it turned out, she could not, as before, work at the university hospital. Her brother was forced to end his medical practice, her sister couldn't study medicine, and her youngest brother's career in the army was over. Her Aryanization should have prevented this, but it turned out that Bormann had deliberately overlooked making this effort on her behalf—possibly, Junge speculates, because he had made failed advances on the dietician. When Hitler was informed of this oversight, by Junge, to Bormann's humiliation, the Aryanization went through, and the von Exners returned to their lives. Within months, the Allies had liberated Vienna.

~

If I had lunch with Hitler, I would want to be more like von Exner than Bormann; I want to think that I would have, in this blessedly hypothetical scenario, the courage to be indignant. I don't like to think I could have a pleasant talk with Adolf Hitler, or that I could bear his presence long without at least being critical, even brutally honest, but if we could somehow meet at a dinner party or reinforced bunker, and I couldn't help interacting with him, I might well behave as I do when faced with anything I consider worth protest. I am afraid I would act like I do in all awkward encounters: evade the points of contention between us, downplay our differences, be polite, avoid a scene.

I would know how to break the ice. I could ask Hitler what he thought of meat. I could mention how unnecessary it is to touch the stuff, when there is so much good cabbage in the world waiting to be eaten.

Hitler and I might nod in agreement over carrot sticks, as I did all I could to deflect his troubling remarks on Jews and homosexuals. If we did I would wonder if, by keeping my objections quiet, I betrayed those who, in my position, couldn't possibly contain their disgust for him. I would sit with Hitler and wish I could find the words to silence him, or make him pause and reconsider his positions concerning, among other things, Russians. Instead we would talk about our favorite salads. I would sing the praises of chickpeas, and worry that, by discussing food instead of his atrocities, I might be doing something unforgivable. My deference to the monster would be an affront to all the people braver than I, who gather at meals and say whatever they please.

58

THE MOST LIFELIKE THING IN THE ROOM

When I told my parents I had become a figure model, at the age of twenty-two in southeast Ohio, they were proud of me and said I was handsome. Then I explained that it didn't mean I was good-looking. It meant I was willing to take off my clothes for other people.

My transition to being a figure model from being no kind of model was quick. I saw flyers posted in town announcing a need for models, had a brief phone conversation with an art school secretary, and showed up to a recruitment meeting. So did three teenage women. I had to fill out an application that asked for a brief description of my body; I wrote that I had no tattoos, and that I was covered with a thin layer of hair.

The recruiter, a polite, nervous man with tattoos on his arms and a thin layer of hair, wanted us to know what we were getting ourselves into. He explained what a typical art class would consist of: up to twenty students, a professor to give us instructions. We would, he emphasized, have to take off all of our clothes, and when he said this I laughed. I didn't know why. Wanting someone to laugh with me, I looked to the teenagers, but they were staring forward, looking unamused and terrified. I understood, then, that I might be the only one present who would have no problem undressing for others, that discussing this activity might make the women uneasy, that after a man tells some college students of the sex opposite mine that they will need to strip for money, their side of the room is the wrong place to point my gaze. I looked away.

~

When I arrived to the art classroom for the first time, and knew that in ten minutes I would be seen naked by a lot of people, my penis got smaller—smaller than it had been when I looked at myself naked in the mirror that morning, hoping to make a good impression. It was failing me at the moment I most wanted it to be itself. I wasn't there to impress; I was there for money, but still I didn't want to be misrepresented, by the most important one of my imminently visible reproductive organs. It was like my body was lying to people, and I couldn't make it stop. I am unaware of an equivalent to this for women who model for artists, but I know they also get nervous, whether or not it has an outwardly notable effect on their anatomies.

I was expected to undress behind a partition in the corner. The momentary privacy it offered seemed absurd. I knew the same body that stripped behind it would soon be on its other side, in plain sight. Shielding my stages of nakedness from the eyes of others was done with a willful ignorance, I thought, of the fact that thirty of those eyes would be on me soon, and that their looks would be critical and unashamed. I emerged from behind the partition, where in place of clothes I had wrapped a bathrobe around myself, with a belt. Students trickled into the room. They knew why I was there; they had never seen me before, and I wasn't wearing shoes or clothes.

Soon I stood in my robe, in the center of the room, as the professor gave instructions to the students. Papers rustled. I untied my belt. I tried to make eye contact with someone, and as soon as I did I knew it was the wrong thing to do. The girl I chose to befriend in this way did not return my smile, but instead glanced nervously at everything that was not about to expose itself to her.

I didn't know how to behave. I had never been in a circumstance like this, and I was never the focus of so much attention. I stood, surrounded, my heart pounding, and tried to act casual.

There is no established polite way to tell someone to remove his clothes, but I knew what the professor meant when he looked at my face and nodded. In a flash I was naked and cold, with my robe on the floor beside me. I kept my eyes pointed low, so as to not embarrass the students as they surveyed my body. Each one focused on my foot or my neck and ran a charcoal pencil across a page I could not see.

~

The work of figure modeling consists of poses. The model is always standing, sitting or sprawling out, in limb arrangements that are interesting to draw. I was asked, sometimes, to stand for an hour at a time, with infrequent breaks and joints that wanted to buckle. At other times I was asked to lay face-down on a sheet for a solid hour, which meant I was being paid to do in public what I did at home for free.

The initial poses of a drawing session, though, are gesture poses. They are taken in quick succession, and held no longer than a minute each; while they last, students must race to draw the whole model. To take these poses I had to make myself a unique mess of lines and dramatic contours. I had to twist and stretch my bone and muscle. I might begin by standing with arms stretched high, and neck arched back—then, a minute later, turn ninety degrees, double over and grab my knee with both hands. I never moved like this in other rooms and buildings.

I had to concentrate, so much that I could sometimes forget altogether the ones who watched me. Other times I was self-conscious, and worried they might criticize my dry skin.

When gestures ended I was pouring sweat, and everyone could see it. My joints felt like nails were driven into them, but the good news was that soon I could sit in a longer, easier pose, or even recline for half an hour. I couldn't help but relax and be thankful for the relief, even though I was still naked in front of a lot of strangers.

~

In an essay, James Baldwin mentions that as a young man he modeled at a New England artists' colony. Claude McKay, Jamaican poet of the Harlem Renaissance, worked as a figure model in Paris. The rooms he appeared naked in were so cold that he contracted influenza. In his autobiographical novel *Impossible Vacation*, Spalding Gray's protagonist models for an art class but is asked by someone in charge to wear a jockstrap.

In *Human Smoke*, Nicholson Baker quotes the diary of Mary Berg, an artist who lived in the Warsaw ghetto. She describes the young people who would wait in line to model for her art class, to be paid with bread. One of the models ate half of what she'd earned and saved the rest for her brother. This model is a hero, an intrepid breadwinner who rescues her loved one from starvation.

While I understood that I didn't model to save anyone—least of all other people—I thought, privately, that since my work was daunting, by doing it I proved how brave I could be. I knew modeling wasn't for everyone; I knew most people would be unwilling to do what I was up to, on campus, for about three hours each week. I felt that a nude model would need to be courageous, and willing to do what most would never dare.

I was surprised, then, to learn from an artist friend that "People don't really like figure models." She explained, "Most people think they're kind of dumb. And annoying." She had overheard me telling someone about my job, outside the classroom, and had pulled me aside to give me this information.

I had heard art students complain about models. One had told me about a woman who disrobed and spent a whole class complaining, when she was supposed to be still and silent. I heard about a man my age, who announced to a class that no one should be put off by his body, that they should talk to him if they felt like it, that he was ready to be friends with them, as he stood before them naked.

When I heard about these people, I thought they were exceptions, that on the whole figure models were upright, dutiful, serious people who didn't feel inclined to tell their audiences how social they were. According to my friend, though, this was how she perceived most figure models, and it was how others saw me when I told them what I did for extra food money.

Still, I was convinced that my work was noble and good. I wasn't being paid well enough to really justify the long hours of pain, of limbs fallen asleep and exposure of my most private parts. I modeled for the money, partly, but moreso to enable the students' educations.

I was doing it for them. I sacrificed hours of my life for strangers who needed a good man to draw, and I never doubted that each moment I spent perfectly still in the nude, acting like a thing that couldn't talk or think, was worth it.

~

It was not lost on me, as I kept still for the strangers, that people do not typically direct their gazes at others the way the students pointed theirs at me. It would have been inappropriate to look at me with such intent and concentration at a restaurant, or out in the hallway, but in the classroom my job was to invite the unabashed, incessant attention of everyone in the room. When I stripped off my robe, I forfeited whatever, in other circumstances, made my body off-limits to probing stares.

The sort of look my body absorbed in art classes was usually given not to people but to things. I often felt, in the classroom, like I should be made of plastic or wood, rather than skin. I was not allowed to move or talk or otherwise bask in my sentience. I would struggle to keep my limbs in place, as my flesh, it turned out, wanted always to shift, to find an easier way to slump against the platform where I froze. My body's effort to adjust itself and my constant breathing reminded me, and them, that I lived after all, but at the same time I had never behaved so much like my own inevitable corpse, or like a table or a chair, or a mannequin.

Whenever I took the rare pose that didn't hurt, I felt like I was becoming a part of the surface I rested on, another mute extension of the room. Minutes stretched into hours, so that it often seemed the pose would never end and I would be there for good, getting rendered indefinitely, in drawings without conclusions.

The drawing room had lots of real objects in it, like easels, chairs, metal poles I held for certain poses, wooden blocks the size of small art students—even a white, plastic mannequin. So long as I was posing, I acted like another of the room's inanimate things. I breathed, and during long poses I shifted because of the pain in my legs or my back, but these were problems; they never added a charming human touch to my presence. The class had to contend with my need to be at ease. I aspired to behave as though I felt and thought nothing, to be

63

more couch than man.

Of course, it would have been cheaper for the art school to forego hiring me and have students draw their mannequin, so the usefulness of drawing a body must have had something to do with this tension between its status as a living thing and its owner's attempt to pretend otherwise. When I modeled I portrayed myself as lifeless, and it was the performance everyone drew. I acted like something that can't feel pain or wonder how big the universe is; they rendered that fiction onto paper.

~

When I started modeling, I didn't have a robe I could bring to work, so I had to buy one. At a department store I found a navy blue bathrobe that seemed ideal. There was no point judging it by whether it kept me warm or made me look strong, as I would wear it solely for its removal. I thought it would be a handsome thing to take off of my body.

The bathrobe was made of thick cotton, and was too big to fit into the backpack I carried. On a day when I modeled I walked around all day with the robe underneath one arm. No one ever asked why I had it with me.

One afternoon, after modeling all morning, I was having coffee at a little establishment with big windows. It was bad coffee, and I must have been distracted by how bad it was, because later that night, at home, I discovered I had misplaced my robe. I couldn't think of where I had left it. A week later, in the same coffeehouse as before, I glanced up from my work to see the bathrobe hanging from a chair at a nearby table. It took me a second to recognize it, but there it was, my prodigal robe. I thought someone must have seen me leave it a week before and held onto it, then quietly placed it near me when she saw me return. I felt like I was being watched. It didn't help that I had spent all morning in a drawing classroom, being watched, and copied onto paper.

~

After my first year as a figure model, I started appearing in John's classroom. I had modeled for several art professors by then. One was tall and calm, with white hair and a moustache; another wore a beret and always played the same Herbie Hancock CD—"Cantaloupe Island" and other tunes—on a stereo. I appeared in John's classes most often, though—usually once a week, sometimes twice. I earned hundreds of dollars from this. It was as pivotal to the effort to keep myself fed as it was detrimental to the well-being of my joints.

John had a lazy eye. Once, when a student accidentally drew my eyes as though they pointed in opposite directions, John pointed at me and told him, "His eyes aren't like that. Mine are." He was short and must have been just over thirty. He was loud. He was friendly to me when I first met him, but as soon as he introduced himself, as I stood in my bathrobe and waited to disrobe, he paced the room and shouted at his students. It was their first day drawing. He said, "I don't want you in here if you're here to fuck around with pencils." He told them they were there to work, and as I watched their faces in an effort to avoid watching his I could tell they had not expected the tirade.

John made me nervous, but something in his military approach was reassuring. Clearly he took his job as seriously as I took mine; he saw the importance of what we were doing, and wanted the students to comprehend it too. He put as much pressure on them as they put on me, whenever they examined my limbs and torso, and I thought by drilling his students like this he might also be trying to frighten the ones who had signed up for the class just to see strangers take off their clothes.

One afternoon, John asked me to sign a release form, and at the end of class his students took turns photographing me. I didn't get to see the photos they took of my naked body until I attended an art show, months later. I had befriended some of the students by then, and they invited me to the show, but didn't tell me what it consisted of.

I was there for half an hour before I figured out that a student had cut images of me from several photos and pasted them onto his canvases, incorporating me as a part of his thesis project. I saw there was a man in some of his paintings, but I didn't recognize him until I caught sight of one in the corner, in which he had blown up and set in the background a face that I slowly understood was mine. First I recognized my eyes. Then I looked around and saw that I was on every frame, in various sizes and oddly posed, with arms stretched out, or knees bent.

Someone told me, "Rob, I think you're his muse."

Something like this had happened before, when I first moved to Ohio. At the time, I wore a full beard. Then, on the first morning I woke in my one-bedroom apartment, my beard felt suddenly wrong. No one in town knew me, and I wanted the people to see me as I really was, without this extra hair on my skin. I scraped it off with a razor.

I hadn't seen my beardless face for months, and I no longer recognized it. Once the hair was gone, from my eyes to my neck I was a stranger. I thought I looked like a woman. I saw, at last, what others must see when they see my face for the first time. I had never felt so out of place in my own skin, and I didn't recover from the estrangement for days.

Figure modeling reproduced this effect, in a subtle way, every time I did it. Standing, sitting or sprawling there at the center of the room, my image was grafted onto more than a dozen sheets of paper, simultaneously. Some renditions were faithful, but in some sketches I didn't look like me at all, and if one judged by the content on the pages I could have been anyone up there. I wanted to come across unmistakably—as though my image, drawn by someone else, could be my signature. I wanted to be definite, but the artists showed me that I could be split into two dimensions and parceled out among them ad infinitum.

~

Some students drew badly. In a memorable sketch, my torso appeared to be one foot longer than it really was. I looked inhumanly skinny, like a naked cartoon.

Once when I modeled for a graduate class, a student drew me in a way that compelled the others to creep behind her easel and snicker, until the professor joined them, burst into guffaws, and said, "You misjudged the proportions a little there." The artist looked at me, sheepishly, over and over. She was stationed in my line of sight. No one told me what was funny, but they left me enough clues to figure out that she had exaggerated my penis to where it looked an absurd, unreasonable size.

Some students, on the other hand, were excellent artists who depicted my body with horrific accuracy. Once, a student behind me

66

rendered some loose fat I had not realized I wore just above my hips. She had made plain my unsightly extra skin, one of my unknown flaws, and had failed to depict me the way I envisioned myself. I stood in my robe through the five-minute break and squeezed my lower back to confirm her appraisal. She had drawn my imperfection with merciless perfection.

I was often surprised by how calm I looked in drawings, though, even when I came out looking fat. I was always staring forward, mouth shut, no anxious concern in my eyes. Even on a day when I was stressed out, in two dimensions I looked placid, or even overcome by a sense of well-being.

~

In the occasional seated pose, my foot would fall asleep and turn purple. Once, I spent thirty minutes with my face buried in my folded arms, and for some reason I started gagging. Some poses were more relaxing than others, but the case was rare that I could stay in one for twenty minutes and not come out of it in pain.

My worst suffering as a model, though, occurred apart from my ankles and knees. The moment was far worse in which I discovered that my daily life consisted of sequential chunks of time spent doing unpaid model work. Whatever crossed my mind in the classroom would cling to me after I dressed and went home. The backache I acquired there returned to me when I sat, silent, among friends. Miles from the drawing classroom, I would sit immobile for ten minutes, because people behave that way, in the car, or in a waiting room. For a few long moments, at home, I would sit still with an avocado sandwich in my hand, and discover that although I had no audience, and I was in clothes, I had essentially just been posing, without compensation.

~

When gesture poses ended, the students would pick one sketch to turn in for a grade, but the rest of their work they disposed of. I would stand in my robe, catching my breath and sweating from gestures, as a roomful of people took down their drawings, crushed them to handfuls of so much paper, and threw them in the trash. Once I considered asking if I could keep some of the drawings, but then I thought of what a vain impulse that would seem to be.

Acquaintances were always surprised to find out I was a figure model. "And you're so shy," they would say, incredulous. I wanted to tell them what it felt like to expose my body to others. I wanted to describe the tension in the classroom at the start of a class, the apprehension of the students. I had stories ready.

I had thought my job would yield infinite conversation, myself at its center always. I found, though, that when I told a modeling story someone would steal the focus back from me. Friends would tell their own jokes, saying, "If I ever tried to be a nude model I'd think about girls and get excited," or, "I bet more people have still seen me naked than you." They talked about modeling as they drew attention from the only one present who had done it. I became secondary to their opinions, to their surprise at what a low wage I earned, and the conversations escaped me.

A student once drew me for forty minutes as I sat for her class, but rather than take her drawing home she left it behind. Each time I returned to the room I saw her image of me on an abused sheet of paper, bunched up in the corner where no one else noticed. After a while I saw it on the floor under the sink, and it stayed there for months. Every time I modeled, I told myself I should retrieve the drawing after everyone left, and take it home with me, but I never did. Someone else finally threw it away.

BOXES

Where is he who seeing a thousand men useless and unhappy, and making the whole region forlorn by their inaction, and conscious himself of possessing the faculty they want, does not hear his call to go and be their king?

—Ralph Waldo Emerson, "The Young American"

On the fourteenth story of an office building in downtown Cleveland, a paralegal named Lars and a lawyer sat at a conference table with me and a half-dozen others, to explain why they had hired us to be their temporary legal assistants. Their firm, Lars said, stood in defense of a beleaguered financial entity that was supposed to have refunded a lot of people, several hundred dollars each, when they refinanced their mortgages. The company hadn't followed through with the refunds. It now faced a class-action lawsuit. This was my first day as a legal assistant, and I was compensated for my training, so as they talked I did my best to determine how much money I would be paid for trying to pay attention to them.

The lawyer, who had the face of Dwight Eisenhower, explained that class action suits are frivolous things instigated by greedy lawyers. In nearly every case, he said, the lawyers get rich while the ones they represent are given maybe a hundred dollars, typically much less. He was enjoying himself. I could tell he didn't often get to talk about work with people who weren't his colleagues. My father was a lawyer, and I recognized in this stranger his enthusiasm for his job.

After the meeting, which I must have made twenty dollars from attending, Lars, a tall man with ears like handlebars, who had shaved his head, emphasizing the size of his ears, escorted us two stories up, to an office on floor sixteen that consisted of several rooms with a dozen cardboard boxes in them. Its carpet was stained several colors. Ceiling panels were missing. The walls were bare.

We legal assistants unfolded tables and chairs that had been set against an undecorated wall, and each brought a box over beside us. Our task was simple, Lars explained. We were to delve into the boxes, and sort through mortgages and other documents that accompanied the purchase, insurance and refinancing of houses, in search of the word "reissue." We were to mark each page, with a red or blue tag, where "reissue" appeared—always obscurely, usually in permanent marker across the low, right corner of a sheet of paper. Then we would return each file to its box, and move on to the next box. Our jobs would last as long as the boxes kept coming. There were, Lars assured us, many more on their way.

Several things were clear. One was that my three years of experience teaching college-level English courses were comically irrelevant to my current position as a legal assistant. Also, I had made some significant errors.

The greatest of these, I knew already, was having moved to Cleveland, one week prior. I had ended an unhappy relationship in southeast Ohio, then quickly gotten serious with another woman, Aurora, who had made it plain that to love her would entail accompanying her when she moved to Cleveland, where she had once lived with her ex-husband and his parents. I acquiesced. I thought it would be an adventure, to move away for love and let it transform my life. I had never lived in a city the size of Cleveland.

We settled downtown, in a loft that had been fashioned out of an old tile factory. Prior to moving in, I had pictured us meeting new people, drinking with them, laughing and carrying on in the heart of this city of two million. But the other residents of our building seemed universally shy, or simply not interested in talking to us. Aside from me and Aurora, they appeared to be the only ones living downtown—

except, of course, the scores of homeless men and women I saw on the streets, in warm and in lethally cold weather.

Having always lived in small towns, even if they were depressed towns with their shares of poverty and homelessness, it was a new experience for me that whenever I walked outside, within one or two minutes of my exposure to the open air, someone asked me, aggressively, for change. I got used to it fast and learned to ignore requests for my attention on the street, but some of the other legal assistants were terrified of strangers who accosted them.

The coworkers most frightened by panhandlers were Chris and Brian, two recent college graduates who had grown up in Cleveland's suburbs. They had played football in high school and college, and together must have weighed five-hundred pounds. Each one standing over six feet tall, their upper bodies alone were the size of small, whole people. One morning, early in our acquaintance, Chris returned from lunch shaken. He said, "My god, did you see that homeless lady? She was standing in the middle of the sidewalk and she got up in my face and asked me for money. I'm like, 'I'm not gonna give you money!'"

I wish I could say that my attitude was better, that I gave money more often to those who asked for it, or—vastly more productive—volunteered at one of the two homeless shelters that stood within a block of my apartment building. But my response was much like Chris's, except that when I refused to help the homeless I didn't talk about it later. Like the suburbanites I would observe when I went to lunch, I would walk across the street to get a sandwich and maintain a neutral, unfazed expression. I would don the same expression when I walked home to the loft ten blocks away, and again when I returned to work in the morning.

~

Although I lived in safety and perpetual warmth, in my loft, like the homeless I did not own a house. Unlike some of them, I had never in my life owned a house, or insured one, or looked at a mortgage, so that the boxes and what I found in them at work were new to me.

Every box was stuffed, predictably, with files. Every file contained a mortgage, a HUD document, insurance forms, ESCRO documentation, floor plans, and photocopied checks. All of it looked important; had I ever wanted to be an identity thief, I thought, this sixteenth floor would have been the place to start. Through the files entrusted to me, I had access to names, addresses, social security numbers—and, in some cases, photocopied credit cards—belonging to hundreds of people who owned houses in Ohio. Although on most days I socialized only with Chris and Brian, I learned a lot about scores of other people through their files.

Every file contained a photocopy of someone's driver's license, but the faces on most of them had not survived Xerox machines. Features were reduced to ink smears. In each photo I could see a mouth and some hair, usually some eyes, but all else was a blur.

One exception was the license of Gary Molnar, a stranger to me. When I found his file, I knew at once where I could find him, if I wanted to make his unsolicited acquaintance. His address was printed on half the pages in his file. I could visit him at home and introduce myself, or come to his house and do something awful, like shove him to the ground.

But I could be less direct in my misanthropy than that. I could go and stake out the DMV at about the time Gary's license was set to expire. When he went to renew it, I could intercept him. Recognizing his face from his unusually crisp license photo, I could sidle up beside him in line and make small talk, pretending our meeting was by chance when in fact I had planned it for months.

I do not know what I would have done then. I might have let on that I knew more about him than I ought to. I might have shoved him to the ground.

Many unsuspecting homeowners were, like Gary, at my fingertips. They were at the significantly larger fingertips of Chris and Brian, too, and there were still other legal assistants scrutinizing files of their own. From up on the sixteenth floor, the homeowners represented in the boxes looked naked to me.

Those who did not look naked to me included the men I passed on my way into the building, who spent every morning, or at least every weekday morning, lying on the sidewalk, wrapped in blankets. They were probably there on weekends as well, but I had the luxury of frequently leaving the city, with Aurora, to visit her family, key members of whom lived a two-hour drive away, in the middle of Ohio, amid wild trees and fresh air.

~

The boxes we sorted through on floor sixteen couldn't reach us until the plaintiffs' team of legal assistants went through them. They stuck their own red and blue tags to the pages they liked, and sent them to a document service to have them copied. When I opened a box, therefore, its contents were already thoroughly marked with red and blue stickers, jutting out of the folders. Because of the tags, it was clear to me, Lars and the others what information the other team sought, on the opposite side of the class action suit. We could see which pages they thought were worth reproducing. I didn't know if this insight was helpful to the firm I worked for, but it made me feel like our opponents were doomed, like we had access to essential details of their methods— meaningless as they were to me.

Elsewhere on the sixteenth floor, just a few doors down, on the adjacent side of the square, was an office that people walked in and out of all day, on their way to the restrooms, and on their way to lunch. They looked like temps to me, because aside from me and my coworkers only they, of the people in the building, weren't invested enough in their jobs to dress up for work.

Lars mentioned that these other temps were the ones who marked the boxes before they came to us. They were the ones who had been hired by our opponents, the plaintiff lawyers. Their firm was housed elsewhere in Cleveland, but because, Lars said, our building leased the cheapest offices downtown, the temps who riffled through these same boxes for our nemeses were not even a hundred feet from us during business hours.

When walking past their office on some mornings, I could hear their supervisor, a woman nothing like Lars, who had lots of hair and an apparent chip on her shoulder, shouting at the enemy temps and carrying on. Chris and Brian noticed her too. Among ourselves we traded stories, and praised Lars for being so tolerant and fair a paralegal.

~

Every night I went swimming at the indoor pool of a YMCA two blocks from my apartment building, about eight blocks from the building I worked in. I would linger in the hot tub and in the steam room that adjoined the locker room, and so did Dean, a man twice my age. He said he worked for a security company. I fascinated him. He would catch up with me and talk my ear off about politics and jobs he wished he had. When I told him where I worked, he was jealous. He said, "I've been trying to get a job with them for years. They never hire me, and you got a job first try? You've got a nice setup there! Nice!"

I thought he must have had my job confused with a different job, as my job didn't exist until I had it. It was temporary. I thought Dean, who had a tendency to misspeak, must have meant that he wanted a job similar to mine, a job that was white-collar, even if it was dull. I didn't know what to say to Dean, except that I would let him know if someone quit.

~

The defense team wasn't striving to win the class action suit so much as they aimed to make the plaintiffs lose. There were multiple ways they could accomplish this. One was to drag the case out for so long that the plaintiffs ran out of money, or had spent so much money on legal fees that winning would no longer gain them anything.

I gathered they had resorted to this strategy the day Lars announced that we were working much too quickly. We had been on the job for a mere two weeks, and had sorted our way through hundreds of boxes. There were only so many hundreds more for us to search, "So everybody slow down," he said. "We've got plenty of time to work on this, and the slower you go the longer the job lasts. So let's relax, take it easy, and just slow it down. Slow it down."

Before Lars's speech, I had been tearing through boxes, marking up probably twenty of them in an eight-hour shift, maybe more. After the instruction to decelerate, rather than burn through files, I would get through five or six a day, sometimes as few as two or three. This left me plenty of time to do whatever I liked, as long as I didn't leave the office. I brought index cards to work, and when Lars was gone—which he was, most of the time—I would work on the book I was trying to write, while Chris and Brian talked about sports.

Unless someone had recently asked one of them for change, sports were all that Chris and Brian talked about. They talked Browns, Cavaliers, Indians. Our radio was tuned constantly to an AM sports talk station. On a local program, for several hours of every day, a man spoke at length about Cleveland's teams, even those whose sports were not in season. Another national sports program lasted from the morning well into the afternoon. We had, in our room, the office's only radio, so that the women who worked in the room next to ours were left to talk to one another, or work in silence.

Although as many women worked on the project as men, I rarely saw them. Temps were divided unofficially according to gender, and members of the opposite sex were on the other side of a wall. We didn't visit them, and they never came to say hello.

My fellow men in the room could not figure out why this was. Chris would say, "They sit over there all the time, and I hear them talking. They never come in here. Why don't they come in here?" The longer the job lasted, the more resentful he grew. He would glare, and throw paper clips at the table—gently but deliberately. He would stand and storm out of the room, shoving his chair against the table.

I knew why the women didn't talk to Chris and Brian. Whenever a woman greeted them, the two giants froze and stared at the floor. When a lawyer—always a man—came up from downstairs to check on us, they would light up and act like instant friends, but if a woman addressed them they could not communicate. I hadn't seen anything like it since high school.

The only thing that froze me in my tracks the way the presence of a woman did Chris and Brian were the isolated hairs I would find, on rare occasions, between two pages in a manila folder. I found a long, red one on a Tuesday afternoon. I could not help but wonder whose it was, what its prior owner's face looked like, and how the hair arrived there, to be exhumed years later by a stranger. Uncertain what to do with it, I put it back.

Once, Chris found a page where someone had accidentally photocopied her fingers at the edge of a document, where she had held it against the glass. When he showed it to me we shared a few seconds of silent wonder, and I asked what he thought the woman with those fingers might be doing at the moment when we found the image of her hand. I don't recall his answer.

~

New shipments of boxes arrived several times a week. None of us tried to keep up with them.

Chris prided himself on his capacity to be at work and do no work. From across the table I watched him peel away fingernails with his teeth, draw pictures, read the newspaper, read men's magazines, and play with the rubber fingertip covers that were meant to make it easier to flip through pages. Sitting across from me, he did nearly everything a person could do that was not work. He said, repeatedly, that he wanted to bring a TV to work with him, and put it just above my head. He said he would watch it all day if he could.

The boxes piled up in the adjoining room where Lars worked, until they formed a cardboard bulkhead. As more of them came in, we started putting them in the other room with the women. When space ran out in there, we lined our walls with new boxes. Soon, the office was so full of boxes it was hard to walk into a room without running into boxes. When Brian wanted to relieve himself, I had to leave my chair so that he could get out of his spot by the window and go to the restroom in the hall. It was like we were in the same row on a cardboard airplane.

Each box weighed a ton, it was so full of papers, so that the longer the boxes remained with us the more they wore each other out. A box at the bottom of a stack of six others was warped and broken after weeks of strain against gravity. The boxes suffered damage simply by bearing our scrutiny, or by bearing the weight that came with waiting for it.

~

For a week, Lars disappeared. He vanished not into the ether but into Akron, forty miles south, in order to find more boxes that he said we would eventually have to rummage through. He said—as if to ensure that while he was gone we would do even less work than we had been doing—that no one was likely to check on us. The Eisenhower lawyer

76

may come to see us, he said, but probably not. So for most of the week of Lars's absence, those of us in the room of men did nothing.

Because I have a capacity for shame, I couldn't help but work a little—I think I got through three boxes in five days—but Chris and Brian didn't open a single one. They listened to the radio and stared forward. After Monday and Tuesday passed, it was clear that Lars had not been kidding about no one checking in with us, so I started bringing a book with me, and more index cards.

~

One morning, it was announced on the radio that a large bank somewhere had apologized for having once accepted slaves as material goods, and had set up a scholarship for African-American students in the South. On ninety-something FM in Cleveland, this was unacceptable. A woman called the morning show and told some energetic DJs, "I'm tired of having to apologize over and over again for slavery, for something that happened two-hundred years ago and I had nothing to do with."

Chris spoke up, then, saying, "I can't wait until our dogs learn to talk, and start demanding we make up for all the things we do to them."

I wrote these statements down on an index card.

~

One of the perks of having my job was that I could make my own hours. I could show up late, or even halfway through the day, and Lars didn't seem to mind. I could work late, and remain in the office for several hours after five o'clock. Lars was gone then, and I could get away with doing nothing, and still be paid, without even having to maintain the appearance of working. No one would be there to see whatever it was I did or didn't do.

I took up the practice of remaining in the office at night, long after everyone had gone home. I would bring a book to work, pretend to work all day, then, after everyone left, drop the pretense of working and simply read. At an hour when I finally had control of the radio, I would listen to Cleveland's NPR station.

Aurora supported this behavior. She worked the late shift at an insurance company in the suburbs, answering phones and addressing complaints well into the night. As long as she was working, she thought I might as well continue working, too.

But I barely worked in the daytime, and at night there was no one even pretending to keep me busy. After a few nights of extended non-work, I found I couldn't bring myself to hang out and read, to make something of the hours I spent not working but being paid to be there anyway. I would pace around the office for an hour to the tune of "All Things Considered," but I thought all the while of other places I could be, where I might feel like I had a purpose. I didn't know where those places were, but if I had I would have gone to one with haste.

Hanging around after work, on an otherwise empty story of this office building that almost never had many people in it, at an elevation that afforded a view of downtown, I looked out on the many empty office buildings that neighbored mine and felt as if I were hanging around a movie theater after the credits had started rolling, when everyone else who had a choice in the matter was already gone.

I knew, though, that I was lucky to feel this way indoors. When the sky grew dark, and the frozen city lit up below me, I could see, across Ninth Street, from my window, a handful of men and women standing in a small park. They bore no evidence of having jobs, houses, or heavy coats. It was the dead of winter in Cleveland, and I remember that before the year was through a man died of exposure, one night, somewhere in the city. I heard about it on the radio.

JAMES AND THE GIANT NOISE VIOLATION

In a few months I would move to Columbia, Missouri, to go back to school. My girlfriend Aurora wanted to move with me, so we went there, for a day, to find a place to live. We met with Keith, a landlord, to see a brick house on a dead-end street, where a row of mostly uninhabited houses ended with a set of railroad tracks. The house was surrounded by low-hanging trees. On the front lawn, a bush shot up seven feet but sagged dramatically, as if to illustrate the trajectory of someone who attempts a great thing but is pulled to solid ground, despite himself.

Keith was gigantic. Over six feet tall, he must have weighed 300 pounds, and wore a beard so long it reached his navel, as if to illustrate the trajectory of milk, if it spilled out of his mouth onto his body. I suppose he could have looked quaint, with that beard, but because he had no moustache it looked like a piece was missing from his face. He spent our first thirty minutes together explaining that the Nazis were not Fascists but Socialists, and that the worst-ever genocide had taken place not in Germany—as he was certain we believed—but in China. We had done nothing to indicate that this interested us.

Within minutes I knew that Keith was insufferable, with his insistent explanation of warped geopolitics and unsettling, unblinking glare. I would have walked away from him, but he was willing to rent the three-bedroom house for five-hundred dollars a month. As we toured it, Aurora and I spoke under our breaths about the money we would save by living there, and how lucky we were to find hardwood floors in a town where most floors were suffocated by carpets. We signed the lease on the front porch, a corner of which sagged like a weight-bearing frown.

Our business done, Keith resumed his lecture. He explained that the news media are biased against men, asking us, "How many stories do you see on the news about breast cancer? Now how many do you see about prostate cancer? None. There's an imbalance."

Eventually, he also mentioned that someone—a "grad student in mathematics"—lived in the basement of the house. His subterranean dwelling was its own apartment, accessible only through the laundry room we shared, so I didn't get to see it, or meet its occupant. Keith said his name was James. He would mow the lawn, he said, and take care of our maintenance needs.

Satisfied, and eager to get away, we left Keith as soon as we could, and then left town, planning to return four months later and begin our lives in Missouri. In August, I finally journeyed there again, alone; Aurora had decided to stay in Cleveland until November. She wanted to keep her job a little longer, and make some money to ease her eventual passage west.

For the last two hours of the ten-hour drive to Columbia, as I traversed the space between there and St. Louis, I feared for my life. A terrifying wind blew in from the north, so strong that as I sped along the little car rocked and buffeted. I had to struggle to keep the car from veering out of control and landing in the ditch on my left. An hour from St. Louis, out of the darkness, the wind began throwing dry leaves at my windshield. I couldn't see. I thought the Midwest was rejecting me. I thought I would be killed by a tornado.

Instead, I arrived in town at one in the morning, directions to the obscure house in hand. I didn't know anyone there, and I couldn't see a thing. My headlights were the only apparent source of light in the city. The street lights were out, and the pitch-dark homes looked abandoned.

When I found the house and pulled into the driveway, James was there to greet me, shirtless. Tattoos stood out on his chest, like cryptic Masonic symbols, with strange designs in them and human eyes peering out from his skin. His actual eyes, on his face, looked earnest,

80

and I could tell despite the dark that he had a prominent chin. Skinny and tall, with a goatee, he smelled like cheap beer and held a can of cheap beer in his hand. He asked me what I thought of the blackout, but I don't remember my reply.

My red Civic was loaded with several boxes of books, some lamps, a blanket, an air mattress, my laptop computer, and some spices I had bought in Cleveland that I planned to cook with. I was sure they sold the same spices in Missouri, but I had wanted to be prepared. It had not occurred to me, however, that I should bring a frying pan, or a fork.

Just before I moved to Missouri, I lived in a loft apartment in downtown Cleveland, where, every night, sirens wailed three stories below me, trains bellowed in the distance, barges churned their way to Lake Erie, and bottles were broken in the street. Removed, in a day, from this reliable clamor, I didn't trust the quiet city of Columbia. The silence felt ominous. Certain that a tree branch or murderer would crash through my window and kill me, on my first night I drank Miller High Life until I fell asleep on my air mattress, in an empty room with white walls.

On nights to follow, perhaps because I had lived on a third story loft in Cleveland and was used to sleeping at a high elevation, I kept myself stowed in the attic. There were plenty of rooms downstairs—a kitchen, a bathroom, some bedrooms and a living room—but they were strange and vacant. Part of the attic's appeal, I guessed, was that it had only one entrance; if someone were to come in and cut me open, I would at least know which direction he was coming from. Every night, I fought the impulse to take this cloistering one step further and barricade myself against Missouri. I could stockpile canned peas and hide in the attic indefinitely. A couple of weeks passed before I was willing to spend time on the lower floor of the house, and even then I had no interest in Missouri's exterior. I looked to the house for static resistance to the alien mess I saw outside it.

James, however, lived there too—something that was ever more apparent to me as my residence continued. The floor that separated us was thin. Every time he made a phone call, I could hear him talking. When he listened to heavy metal, which he did often, it shook my floor. When he staggered through a classic rock tune on his acoustic guitar,

I was his audience. If James went to the bathroom, it was audible to me, especially when I was in my own bathroom; they were right on top of one another. In September, I gathered that James' girlfriend broke up with him. He spent the better part of a day crying into his pillow, or couch cushion, or bag of marshmallows; his sobs were muffled by something, but I couldn't say by what with any certainty. I wanted to be sympathetic, but it would have been improper to express sympathy, as I wasn't supposed to hear him crying; I knew of his grief merely because the house failed to shelter us from each other.

The next thing I learned about James was that whereas I would have casual drinks with my new friends in Missouri, and even get drunk on occasion, sometimes by myself, James and his friends undertook frequently an altogether different kind of drinking. They had reached another stage, at which consuming alcohol was a serious commitment.

Whenever James had a day off, they would start drinking early in the morning, and continue well into the night. Every time I saw James, he had a beer in his hand or I could smell alcohol on his breath, no matter what time it was in the afternoon or morning. I tried to keep track of his schedule, without going so far as to write it down, but all I could learn was that he rarely slept, and it sounded like he spent more time drinking and listening to music than I spent doing anything.

I also knew that James smoked, constantly, because he did it indoors until I finally complained. The fumes crept through his ceiling and soaked up in my clothes. When his friends were around, they smoked too.

Halfway through October, James developed a terrible cough. When I first heard it, I thought he was throwing up, or choking. Lasting about fifteen seconds at a time, it was a genuine cough, one that came from the pit of his chest, or so I gathered from the sound. It was as if he attempted to expel a live wolverine from his torso, fur and all, but could not quite get it out. He sounded like a stuck drain, if one could cough. He sounded like Gollum.

I thought that if someone were to try to kill me by strangulation, and I could choose the murderer, I would choose James. I would hear him coming from a hundred feet away. He must have coughed twice a minute, every minute he spent awake. Eventually, I came to rely on his cough for a sort of metronomic consistency.

82

In October, Aurora decided she would move to Kansas City, instead of moving in with me. She had grown impatient. Afraid of losing me to the distance between us, she made the perplexing move of arranging for her employer, a large insurance company, to transfer her to an office in a city 127 miles west of me, and much farther away from anyone else she knew.

I flew out to Cleveland, so that we could drive a rented truck full of her things halfway across the country. At the end of three days of loading, driving and unloading, my legs hurt, and I sat on a box of art supplies in a strange city on a Monday night. I was in another foreign place, where the only person I knew was Aurora. She knew only me and, with her distrust of most people, her accusations that I didn't love her, and her persistent, false suspicion that I was in love with my new friends in Columbia, she was in no better shape than I was.

We had stopped at the house in Columbia to drop some things off. One of them was a metal table with its glass surface missing, which she had insisted on keeping, despite the missing surface. Other things were paintings, produced by Aurora before she knew me, when she was still married to an unfaithful man who stole money from her often, who would disappear for days at a time without explaining himself, making subsequent relationships challenging for her. The paintings were large, and most of them depicted her body. One was a five-foot, mostly blue rendering of her naked back. Another was a huge, red image of her pensive face and shoulders. We hung it at the foot of my bed, and Aurora said, half-joking, that her painting kept a close eye on my sheets and anything that might take place between them. After Aurora moved, I was expected to drive the two hours to see her at least once a week. On weeks when I failed to go see her twice, she would question my devotion to her, and be furious.

When I was in my living room and James was in his, even though we were on different levels, it felt like we were in the same room together. If he talked, I could make out most of the words; if he switched on his TV, I knew what he was watching. For my first few weeks in the house I would hear James and expect to turn my head and see him sitting over by the kitchen door, but then I remembered he was a floor below me, and I had no TV for him to watch.

Despite my persistent solitude, one body other than mine and

James' had a constant presence in the house. It was a replica of a German girl Aurora knew before we were together. Aurora had taken a cast of her in Germany, then brought the cast back to Ohio and reconstructed her as a ceramic bust. When she moved to Kansas City, she left this girl with me, along with the paintings. She was glazed white with brown hair painted on her head, a red heart painted on her chest, human hand imprints on her back, and silhouettes of reclining naked men on her torso. I never understood why they were there. The girl's arms were outstretched, palms up, as if in supplication, but her right hand was gone so that one arm ended with a wrist. Her head was uplifted slightly. Her body ended where her legs would have begun, so she looked like she was halfway buried in the floor, as if her legs hung from James' ceiling.

The bust looked sad, maybe even desperate, with her mouth sealed shut and her eyes unblinking. She looked like she was on the verge of tears. Where I had placed her, with her arms held out, it also looked like she was pleading with my bookshelf. She looked enough like Aurora that I could consider her a substitute for my girlfriend, a reminder that she existed and was good at molding people out of clay.

Meanwhile, the real Aurora grew more demanding. I did not visit her enough, she said. When I did, I was not demonstrably happy enough to see her. I was tired all the time and claimed I had work to do. I was not making time for her. I could see her points; my life outside of Aurora was consuming me, and it cost a fortune in time and money to drive to her so often. She told me I didn't earn enough money, that I did nothing to support her.

As things with Aurora worsened, I grew wary of the German girl in my living room. I had been careful all along to not step on her arm and break it, but I was ever more aware of the rage I would face if something happened to this bust, which seemed all the time to more closely resemble my girlfriend, who had such an insistent grudge with me I hardly recognized her anymore. I gave the bust a wide berth, especially on nights I spent drinking, which increased in frequency. There might as well have been a ceramic bowl of nitroglycerin in the corner. I told James and Keith, one afternoon, as they worked in the yard, that my kitchen sink's drain was clogged. That night, James came up in jeans and an old t-shirt to fix it. As he worked, he talked my ear off—whenever he spoke I could not get a word in. He had a voice that filled up the whole house. First he told me I should never mention a problem with the house to Keith, and that I should instead bring it straight to him in the basement. James said Keith had instructed him, "Now you look and you tell me if you see bacon grease coming out of that drain when you unhook it. I told that guy when he moved in not to pour bacon grease down there."

There was no bacon grease, as I am a vegetarian. Keith had still other wrong ideas, and I learned a new one each time I saw him. He thought writers were automatically suspect, guilty in ways they themselves were not aware of, because both Adolf Hitler and Josef Stalin had written books. I heard from one of his other tenants that if you gave him half a chance, he would tell you things like this for up to three hours at a time.

As James fixed the drain, he told me the story of his recent life. He was thirty-three. He had moved to Columbia for college, gotten a degree in mathematics, finished some coursework for a Master's degree in Chemistry, and then taken a break from it—one that was still in effect. He said Keith was letting him live in the basement rent-free in exchange for work, and that he also worked for some other landlords, as a maintenance man. In about five years, he said, Keith was going to give James the whole house as a gift, for all his years of service.

James unfastened my drain, and a mess of wet couscous spilled out of it into a bowl, followed by another mess, of black, chunky stuff that he called bacteria, which he said must have been there before I moved in.

I felt, at that moment, like an interloper. When James took over the house, I imagined, he would probably move out of the basement to the upstairs, where I lived. I was paying rent, but the ultimately rightful owner of the place was James. If I scuffed up the hardwood floor, I was messing up his eventual floor. If I had sex in the bedroom, not only would he hear it; I would be doing it in his eventual room. I didn't know if James felt strongly about this, or even saw it this way, but I got the impression that he did—not from something he told me or shouted to one of his friends, but from his indoor smoking habit, and the way he played unreasonably loud music at hours of the morning such as two. James acted like I wasn't living there. He threw his weight around like he owned the place, and it seemed significant that in the near future he would own the place. If James had been a ghost in the house, trying to expel me by sheer irritation, he would not have behaved any differently.

When James shouted, it was not the kind of shouting that most people do. His voice had an unusual quality, in that whenever he raised his voice and had enough to drink he sounded like he was pleading for his life. If he was telling someone that he liked a certain car, even though the subject was benign, it sounded like he was discussing that car while someone held a knife to his throat. When James was drunk, and spoke at a high volume—two things that always went together for him—he sounded like he was on the verge of tears, or was begging for something to eat.

I, meanwhile, was trying to sleep, read, argue with Aurora on the phone, or consume the better part of a bottle of wine. I must have produced noise, with my feet or my telephone voice, but I never played loud music. I didn't shout. James, on the other hand, had a presence in the whole house, despite his confinement to the basement. Even in the attic I could hear him—talking, shouting, playing his guitar. He was inescapable. He was a part of my life, whether I wanted him in it or not.

One night in November, on my way up from the laundry room James lived next to, he emerged from his apartment and looked at me. I thought there must be a problem, because he never approached me for conversation. He started talking about the furnace, though, which we had just started using. He said, "You know, I didn't think much of that furnace before. But it's going pretty good. I think it's gonna do the job." He kept watching me, without expression, and continued, "I didn't think it was all that strong, but it's going pretty good and I haven't even smelled any old shit coming out of it." I nodded, and told him I was happy with the furnace too. He went back inside, reeking of vodka, and I climbed the stairs, basket of clean laundry in my arms.

A few weeks after our meeting in the basement, I finally dealt with James' having neglected to pay me for the utilities we shared. Each month he was supposed to pay for one third of the water, gas and electric bills, but for three months I didn't hear from him. I left copies of the bills, on schedule, taped to his door, as he had asked me to do when I moved in, but the only sign of him I usually caught was the smell ·

of cigarettes, and his voice as he shouted to his friends. One Wednesday night he cried, emphatically, repeatedly, "Look at my bunghole!" to someone unknown.

Whenever I ran by chance into James, he apologized for not paying me the money he owed. He would say, "Oh man, Rob, I'm sorry, I'll get that money to you in a couple of days, I just got to wait a couple of days to get paid is all."

Eventually, I e-mailed the landlord's wife and explained the situation. On the morning that followed, James knocked on my door once per hour, starting at seven, before I finally climbed out of bed and dressed in dirty clothes to answer him. He walked into the living room, his hands shaking, and told me he was sorry, he would have the money soon.

When James wasn't shouting to his friends, he was often shouting at them. He could not seem to keep them under control, and according to the things I overheard, his friends took advantage of him. They never thanked him for anything. He provided them a place to get drunk, and beer for them to drink, but they betrayed him whenever they could. In an afternoon moment of rebellion, once, a friend of his hummed, nasally, for several minutes. He was loud enough that I could hear him upstairs, while James shouted at him to stop. I don't recall how he resolved this.

At three in the morning, one night in December, James brought his friends home yet again. I woke to the noise of his door swinging hard, and by the sound of his voice I tracked his progress into the basement, through the kitchen, toward his stereo. Within seconds, out came the unmistakable sound of Glen Danzig's first album—guitars, drums, and Danzig's trademark heavy metal voice.

James and I had almost nothing in common. We had different kinds of friends and lifestyles, and we seemed to come from very different backgrounds. Perhaps the only thing we had in common was that we were both familiar with Glen Danzig's first album. I was more conscious of the disparity between us than ever, the night he came home so late and threw a party with his friends. I could not comprehend a man who lived with such reckless disregard for other people—and for himself, for that matter.

The music was so loud, it rattled the frame of my bed. It was as if Danzig himself performed with a full band in my bedroom. My first thought was that I should go downstairs, level with James—literally—and ask him if he would not mind keeping the music down, or off. But it was three in the morning. I was angry, delirious and naked. So I lay in bed for forty-five minutes, passively hoping that James would just stop so that I wouldn't have to ruin his party lifestyle, and we could both win: I could get my five hours of sleep, and he could pass out face-down on his bathroom floor with a smile on his face.

That strategy failed; James and his friends didn't stop their fun for my sake. The music stayed loud, and James was shouting louder than I had ever heard him. It didn't sound like he was even saying words. He and his friends were also stomping their feet, something they hadn't tried before.

In order to discourage this incomprehensible behavior, I pulled my wooden walking stick out of my closet and stomped around the house, banging the stick against the floor. It took a minute of this to elicit a response. Someone turned the music down, and I heard James tell his friends in a hushed voice that this had to be the "last song" before they quit. There was some arguing. I heard James say, "Okay, just a few more songs and that's it, we gotta stop." The music got loud again.

I should have just gone downstairs and spoken to James. But then again, many months later, after I moved out of that house, I met a woman at a craft shop who turned out to have been my next-door neighbor when I lived in the house with James. She knew all about him. She said that one night, a year before I moved in, James had his music turned up high—so very high they could hear it over at her house—so her husband walked over in the middle of the night to knock on James' door and speak with him. James didn't answer. The man returned home, the music continued, and no one got any sleep. Hearing this story made me feel better about the spineless course of action I took, on the night I was faced with a similar problem.

As well-versed as Keith was in genocides bigger than the Holocaust, he didn't have an e-mail address, and I didn't want to call him so late. Instead I wrote an exasperated e-mail to his wife. I told her about Danzig, and wrote that between James' smoking and his constant noise the house was uninhabitable. I knew what effect this might have. I knew James lived below me only because Keith let him stay there. Telling

Keith's wife about James' actions would imperil his living circumstances, and that was exactly what I wanted to do. I wanted him out of there. The music continued through the night, and I didn't sleep until five in the morning.

At eight I woke to more music coming from downstairs, and also to what I can only call emphatic shrieking. James was pissed, in multiple senses of the word. I had no trouble making out what he said that morning; he might as well have spoken to me through an intercom. He shouted to his ever-present friends, "I wasn't playing any fucking music. Goddamnit! I wasn't fucking playing fucking music!" He repeated this many times. I wondered if he believed it. Only three hours had elapsed, but alcohol is a powerful thing. I wondered if James had completely forgotten what he had done the night before, if he had no recollection of Danzig and his own stomping feet.

I heard James exclaim, "That motherfucker," and learned from his clearly drunken remarks that Keith had called him, angry, and told James he was trying to run "a business." I sat at my desk a long time and tried to read. I didn't think anything would happen if James heard me moving upstairs, but I was reluctant to make my presence known. Later, James was saying to his guests—or to me, through the ceiling—"Yeah, Rob, why don't you send a fucking e-mail about that. Send a fuckin' e-mail."

A month later, Aurora sent me an e-mail and told me it was over, we were breaking up, she would soon return to Ohio for good. That night I drank a pint of whiskey. The next day I went swimming and saw a therapist, for the first time in seven years. I told her about Aurora and the year I'd had. She told me I should drink more water, and said that, because I was "soft-spoken," she thought I might be a homosexual.

For weeks, Aurora's belongings remained in the house, including the paintings and the woman with the severed hand. Every time I left the house I walked past a tall, blue canvas that presented in two dimensions the same shoulders I had once been in the habit of rubbing with lotion.

James, meanwhile, procured a cat. He called it "Natasha," and I would often hear him calling for her, between hacking fits, out the back door. I had never heard tenderness in James' voice, but I heard it when he called to Natasha, and when she, after a minute of calling, would emerge from the outside world and elicit from him a sound that resembled cooing.

I arranged with Aurora, silently, by e-mail, to bring her things to her. I rented a van and loaded into it her crates of art supplies, her paintings, her four metal chairs, her rug, her other rug, her Buddha tchotchkes, her books, her cookbooks, and the tampons she had left in my bathroom cupboard. The bust was the hardest thing to move. For months I had been watching her, biting my nails, hoping I never kicked her accidentally, or dropped a box on her head and snapped her neck. Now I had to transport her more than a hundred miles. I wasn't even sure how to pick her up, but I held my breath, grabbed her by her hollow underside, and eased her out onto the truck's passenger seat. We were silent as I piloted the van on the highway, and when we reached Aurora's apartment her creator was relieved to see her unharmed.

After a wordless hour of unloading and lugging things up a flight of stairs, as the sun went down, I sat with Aurora on her red couch and we talked. Her new therapist, she said, had put her on two antidepressants. She added that she had lost fifteen pounds, and that she didn't like her life. At a loss, I told her I was sorry. As I left, I could hear her neighbor, across the hall, wrestling with his daughter and laughing.

After I complained to Keith's wife about James, things were different. He was still a party animal, but at reasonable times of day, when it wouldn't keep me up, like six in the evening or eleven in the morning. At hours when most in our time zone slept, he was the mild-mannered James I preferred. I often heard him leaving in the evening, slamming the door on his way out, and I wondered if he was on his way to drink somewhere else. It was none of my business.

One evening in February, I went down to the basement to start some laundry. James had left his door open, but I could tell he wasn't home because of how unlike cigarettes the house smelled. After I loaded sweaters and sheets into the washing machine, I paused a moment to peer into his kitchen. I saw a cat's dish, on the floor, with half an order of cheese sticks in it.

I admitted to myself that this, too, was none of my business, and retreated upstairs. My interest in James was waning. I didn't feel sympathy for him anymore, and thought the sympathy I felt for him early on must have been condescending—which was made literal by the fact that to reach James I would have to descend a staircase. As long as I lived above James, whether I liked it or not, I was intruding on him. I knew nearly everything he did, and assumed that this knowledge and its concomitant discomfort were mutual.

By the time spring came around, although I had lived in the house for eight months, I felt like I had no home. Some of James' friends had developed a habit of hanging out in a maroon Geo Tracker in the driveway, for the better part of every morning. When I left the house, I would see at least one man—sometimes three men—seated in the vehicle, listless. Sometimes they looked up at me, expressions missing from their faces.

In the spring, Keith let me break my lease without penalty. Having gone through an ugly breakup, having to shoulder all of the rent for a house too big for me, I was in pitiful circumstances, and he could see it. I found a new place to live, one half of a duplex a few blocks from the house.

On moving day, I entered my new place for the first time, a box under one arm, relieved to be escaping the sound of James' voice and the smell of his cigarettes, and found him standing on a ladder in the middle of the living room. He appeared to be replacing a light bulb. I was not altogether surprised by his presence, because I knew he worked for my new landlord in addition to working for Keith. It was understood that if I had a problem with an appliance, or something, James would walk over to fix it. Our relationship would be much like what it had always been, but without all the shouting.

I didn't hear much from James anymore, having left the space where I could hear everything he did all day. Still, I pulled up my blinds one morning, and James was standing out my window, staring off, taking a break from mowing the lawn. As I sat at my desk a week later, facing a different window, out of nowhere James appeared with a hose and sprayed the glass as he looked in and watched what I was doing. It took me a minute to realize he was rinsing the exterior of the house, and was not trying to tell me something by a cryptic, nonverbal gesture.

Often I saw James walking past my new apartment. I spotted him in the maroon Tracker as it passed my window. I was glad that

James was getting out more than he ever seemed to before, because fresh air is good for everyone, but there were times—especially as I sat at my desk, writing about James, and he walked past on his way to do something I would not see or hear—when I felt like I was being haunted.

One night, some friends and I went to a bar that we had never before considered entering. I went to the jukebox, and out of nowhere James stood beside me, asking, "They got any good stuff on here?" We looked at each other, and only then did he discover it was I, his ex-neighbor. Delighted by this chance encounter, he laughed. He explained that he had not known it was me, that he was planning to browbeat me—thinking me a stranger—into choosing songs he liked instead of songs I liked.

He said things were going well with my replacement, that the two of them got along better than he and I ever did. He introduced me to a friend as his "old roommate," which was either disarmingly chummy or presumptuous, I couldn't decide which. As we stood there, Black Sabbath blaring in our faces, after almost a year of listening to each other across a wooden floor, we finally had a conversation. I don't remember the words we spoke, but I hope that no one lived on the level above us and was trying to go to sleep.

SKILLET

When I first moved to Missouri, years ago, I rented a house with an unfortunate neighbor in the basement who spent every evening drinking enough to float a ship and shouting at his guests, who never seemed to leave. Then I moved into an apartment, where I shared a wall with a neighbor who played the drums and appeared to drink with moderation.

If you had broken into my apartment, at that time, in search of electronics and gemstones, instead finding expired condoms and a remarkable surplus of paper clips, you would not have known what to make of my kitchen floor. You could not have missed the deep, inch-long cuts that gashed across the linoleum, giving the impression that I released a wild panther there, then watched its claws dig into the surface as it scrambled to escape through the back door.

The cuts were unsightly. It looked as though I had gotten lost in my kitchen, somehow, and tried to dig my way out with a nail file. I made them by accident, in a spell of mundane negligence, and for many months my landlord did not repair them.

On a Saturday afternoon, in June, I put some water on my stove to boil, in a kettle, and left the kitchen. I was writing something I would later lose interest in, but on that day it was absorbing me. I thought I would hear the kettle and eventually be reminded of the boiling water, so I didn't think about it. When the kettle failed to make a

95

noise, I failed to notice. I forgot about the hot appliance.

After a series of long, distracted minutes, I returned to the kitchen and found that the electric burner beneath the kettle was off. The one behind it was on, glowing bright red, and on top of it was my skillet.

I saw that I had done something stupid. I had switched on the wrong burner, and then, transfixed by an unrelated thing, lost track of time. The pan had been heating for fifteen minutes. Still I thought it would be okay. I had to get the skillet off the heat.

As soon as I lifted it, in all directions the skillet exploded, spraying red across the room. The skillet spat, as though it had been filled with hot oil. Something spilled on the floor. It was turning to smoke. I was still holding onto the skillet, and didn't want to be, but I was too busy dodging hot sparks to throw it. The heat—or whatever it was— hissed at me and something splashed on my sock and burned through to my skin. I tossed the pan in the sink. I tore the sock off my foot. I almost fell over.

I did the thing that felt natural: grabbed some paper towels, wetted them under the faucet, and began scrubbing at the floor. When I scrubbed, something rattled across the linoleum. The stains were not coming out. The smoke alarm went off.

The alarm had never gone off before, so I had not made a plan for silencing it. It was over my dresser, out of reach. I tried to stand on my bed and grab the screeching device, but I fell off. I landed hard on the edge of the dresser with the side of my torso. I doubled over. I could hardly breathe.

I said "Fuck," in a tone of voice that I knew would convey to the empty room what I was feeling. For an instant I thought of my mother, in her kitchen in Wheeling, doubled over and also saying "Fuck" as she stubbed her toe, or accidentally burned herself. It was one of the many things I heard her say when I was growing up, and it was exactly what I did that very second, only I was in Missouri, the floor was weeping smoke, and no one was there to watch it happen or hear me.

I stood on my bed again and pulled hard at the alarm, which came off the wall and fell behind the dresser with a sympathetic chirp. I returned to the kitchen, turned on a fan, and opened the back door to clear the air.

96

My first thought, after this ordeal was over, was that it would make my appearance at the wedding I was supposed to leave for in ten minutes significantly less joyous. I had just started dating Stefanie, whom I would later marry, and she had invited me to this wedding, so I had wanted to be in high spirits for the event, or at least spirits that were mid-level and free from the sway of surprise kitchen catastrophes. My next thought was that when my landlord found out what had happened he would be unhappy with me. I had just started renting the apartment from him, and it was clear that the events of that afternoon would not inspire confidence in my capacity to not torch the place.

I stared at the floor. It was streaked erratically with deep burns that had turned brown and were there to stay. I had ten minutes to prepare for the wedding. I was glad it was not my own—not because I feared commitment, but because my nerves were shaken. I was terrified of what my mutilated floor would cost me. I was already nearly totally broke, and I was not yet sure how I would pay my rent that summer.

I put on a shirt and tie. I was pouring sweat. I smelled terrible. My side was red but turning blue and purple from where it hit my dresser. I was shaking, and in five minutes I would leave for an event where I hoped there would at least be something strong for me to drink. As I stood in my roasted kitchen, sweat in my eyes, keys in my hand, the fan blowing smoke out my back door, I was helplessly alone.

~

The wedding turned out to be fun after all, because there was a lot for me to drink—too much, actually. Someone took pictures, and in them I look tired.

When I returned from the wedding trip, I smelled like wedding whiskey and my apartment smelled like melted linoleum. I investigated the stove to see what exactly had happened. Underneath the burner, on the surface of the stove, where the skillet had been cooking for so many minutes, I found a shiny object, a piece of metal about the size of a cell phone. It was shaped something like an enlarged peanut, as it had taken on the rounded contours of the stove's surface. It had a small but deep hole in one side. It was not supposed to be there.

A few minutes later I saw that the base of my skillet—the part that had been in contact with the burner—was scorched. Most of it had worn off completely, leaving behind some brown and black flakes. I saw the connection between these two things. Apparently the pan, heated from the burner I had switched on by mistake, had gotten so hot that it melted. It had turned to liquid and cooled suddenly on the cover of my stove. This shiny metal object, which had seemed to come from nowhere, had previously been a sizable chunk of the base of my skillet; the pieces of metal on the floor were also pieces of skillet, which would have continued to collect on the surface of my stove, had I left the pan where it was.

The skillet piece was useless, barely heavy enough to be a paperweight, but I spent long minutes of the days to follow with my eyes fixed on it. I had created it, so I wanted to understand it.

Most of the metal piece was in the shape of a cohesive 3-D lopsided oval, and it was rather handsome, but its unsettling feature was an appendage that protruded and pointed up, like an antenna. This resulted from the melted metal cooling as soon as it separated from the skillet; it froze in place and took the shape of its own viscous stream. This extra piece rendered the whole object odd-looking and awkward to hold. The antenna sprouted out of the metal piece's side, in an arc that extended a couple of inches and ended at a bifurcated point. It looked, then, like the metal piece had a head, with two horns on it, and underneath what would be the head were two other points that resembled a pair of shoulders. When the metal piece faced a certain way, it appeared as though, with its long, extended head, it was looking at me.

Most of the time, the metal chunk sat on my desk. When it got in my way I moved it to the top of my bookshelf. I would show it to people who came over, but it was rare for anyone to come over.

Some people had nice things to show their friends: my mother had paintings and antique furniture; my brother Sam had a house. I had a melted and resolidified piece of what I thought might be aluminum.

~

When I was growing up, I thought my mother was unreasonable because of the terrible things she thought our lamps were capable of inflicting on us. She would admonish me to always be careful with lamps, because if a light bulb came close enough to a lampshade it would catch fire and burn our house down. She warned me about this every time she saw me turn one on. I was never allowed to have fireworks.

My mother also worried an awful lot about her kitchen. Every single time we left the house—she and I, with two or three of my five siblings—she would ask me, usually after we boarded the station wagon, to go back inside and make sure the oven and stove were off. If she left the house without me, she would call from where she was and ask me or my brother or sister to make sure the stove and oven were turned off. She never owned knives sharp enough even to slice soft vegetables efficiently, for fear a child might grab one and efficiently slice off his or her fingers. A laundry chute on the second floor was nailed shut, to prevent a child from climbing in and dropping two stories to the basement floor. My mother had six children, and the eldest and youngest were born eighteen years apart, so her fears lasted a long time; they were able to thrive and grow over the course of her motherhood. I, a middle child, watched.

My mother has characteristics other than anxiety: she is a talented painter, and she is also smart and funny. But I was not thinking of those qualities after the skillet accident, as I eyed my scorched kitchen floor in a state of panic, wishing, despite my adulthood, that I could call her and tell her this thing had taken place without confirming her persistent fears about what could happen to me at any given moment in the dangerous world.

~

Soon after the skillet accident, the skin on my thumb started peeling. It wasn't coming off in strips, but at the end of my thumb, the part where the thumbprint comes from, little bits of skin were dying and abandoning the rest of me. This was unprecedented. The cause was a mystery, until one Sunday morning when I sat at my desk, holding onto the chunk of metal. I gripped it with my left hand and with my right I plucked its little antenna, like I was strumming it, because it made a soft metallic noise and in an absent way I was fascinated. I had been doing this for weeks before I saw that the antenna was scraping the end of my thumb, flaking off my skin.

The rest of me was, meanwhile, diminishing. One morning, after I went swimming and ate my breakfast of granola and plain yogurt, I found that my weight had dropped from 185 pounds to 170. I had noticed, days before, that my pant legs were dragging on the pavement, but hadn't thought it significant. The weight loss must have happened gradually, but its recognition hit me suddenly, and the loss was accidental. My legs did not look the way they looked a year before, and when I woke in the morning I was greeted with less of a body than I expected.

One of the causes for my loss of body mass might have been similar to the cause for the skillet's dramatic weight loss. It was so hot in Missouri—with a heat index into the hundreds, every day—that if I spent even five minutes outdoors I became a dripping mess of sweat. All summer, when I walked to the swimming pool, walked to the summer class I taught, walked to clear my head after a long morning spent drinking too much coffee, I must have sweated off a couple of those pounds, just as extreme heat melted off a large chunk of one of my more useful kitchen items.

~

I always knew kitchens could be dangerous, but in my post-skillet world I understood what mine was capable of. I knew—as never before—that some misplaced heat could cost me hundreds of dollars, or even burn me, and I thought about it whenever I put scones in my oven, caramelized onions in my replacement skillet, or heated more water for the French press. I was hesitant to raise a temperature, even when it was in my best interests to do so, even when the situation was under control. Often I worried, all of a sudden, at the supermarket or in a classroom, that I might have left my stove on. I wondered, in a way that wasn't worthwhile, if something in my apartment might be burning.

In all kinds of places, many times a day, I had to heat metal to some extreme point or another just to make my world function properly. If I wanted flat clothes I heated a metal plate at the end of an iron. At the Laundromat, lesser extremes of heat made my shirts dry. My little life felt, sometimes, like an overheated mess, a thermal spike that should not be, a subtle bonfire that felt excessive just because it was there.

100

My concern for the temperature did not come from the heat itself so much as it came from the fact that the objects which were heated—my iron especially—were very near to other things not meant to withstand heat. When my skillet exploded, and some of the hot metal splashed out of the kitchen onto the carpet in the adjoining room, the carpet did not stand a chance; the metal burned right through and embedded itself in the floor. Pieces of metal were fused to the carpet, permanent drops of cooled ruin that I saw each time I went to the kitchen to make more coffee. They looked like bulbs of mercury, but they were hard and trapped in a rug.

Post-skillet, I gained some insight concerning why my four brothers and one sister lived within an hour of each other—within sixty miles of the house where we grew up. It is one thing when your skillet explodes and roasts your kitchen and you panic, and you have a brigade of family members who can reach you in fifty minutes in case things really go wrong. It is another thing altogether when this happens soon after you've moved to Missouri and you live alone, and even though you have friends there and your new girlfriend cares about you, you've known not one of them for more than ten months, and there's no way to know for sure that one or two of these good people, upon hearing that you've done this stupid thing, will not privately chalk it up to your being from West Virginia, a state that has stereotypes working against its emigrants. There is no way to be sure that they won't think you're an imbecile, especially if you have inherited your mother's tendency to think paranoid thoughts.

When the summer was nearing its end, and my landlord seemed to still have no plan for fixing the floor and taking care of my mess, and it was so hot outside that I regretted constantly spilling more of my body heat out of my pores and into the atmosphere, I adopted a resentment for the shiny piece of metal. Not only was I using it compulsively to take off small pieces of my own thumb. It was always in the way. There was no place to put it; it didn't belong anywhere, because it wasn't meant to be in the first place. I had a dream in which I visited the family of my ex-girlfriend Aurora: I got uncomfortable, because they didn't like me anymore, so I left, but then I had to go back because I had left the odd piece of metal with them and wanted badly to get it back. I returned to their home, and asked them for it. They were angry.

It was embarrassing. I woke up and still felt embarrassed.

I was upset with the world because of the stuff it was made of. My carelessness notwithstanding, I was convinced that the skillet ought to have been made of stronger metal. Nor did I understand linoleum: as never before, I resented the ease with which it melted. All it took was liquid metal to burn and ruin my kitchen floor.

I wanted the world to be stronger than that. I wanted the pieces of my home and my life to be tougher than they apparently were. I wanted things that would not melt, that would instead withstand my skillet when it ceased to be a skillet and turned to hot liquid. My landlord eventually replaced the scorched linoleum with a strong layer of tile, and that was a step in the right direction, but to this day my days are full of plastic that is asking to be broken.

I often thought that if I died in my Missouri apartment, the most remarkable things that anyone would find among my belongings were an invitation to yet another wedding, which I would not attend, furniture from IKEA, some dry erase markers, and the shiny piece of metal with a stem reaching out of it whose origin would be an utter mystery.

If I died there, I imagined, then surely members of my family would come to Missouri, to clear out my stuff and put it someplace else. I knew which one of my siblings would take home my computer. I knew who would get my car.

If my brother Jim found the ugly piece of metal on my desk, he would throw it away, and so would my brothers Sam and David. So would my father. So would my mother. This would make no difference, if I did not think the piece of metal meant something, if there were nothing of significance I thought I could learn from it. Years after its creation, I sit at my desk sometimes still and let it hang from my fingernail by its stem. I stare at it, and think about nothing.

I am convinced that my family would in no way understand this, that they would not see the value of this useless piece of previously useful metal. I worry that no one else would get it either, and sometimes I know that I am utterly alone in this world.

WE ARE ALL DEALERS IN USED FURNITURE

In the winter of 2009, I took custody of a sword. At thirty-one inches from hilt to tip, it is the longest historical artifact in my house. Etched into its dull blade are an eagle, a shield, some flowers and an "E Pluribus Unum." It once belonged to my grandfather, an emergency room doctor and amateur historian whose collection of Civil War relics was dispersed among my mother and her siblings when he died. I don't know where he found the sword, or who owned it first. My mother told me it was once carried by a Union officer, but now that it belongs to me it is an ornament, not a weapon, a thing meant to be placed on a mantel, not plunged into a Southerner.

Above a mantel, in the home of my aunt Posy, was where the sword hung the night my mother called to relay some of the sorriest news I had ever heard. I was on day three of a three-week stay at an artists' colony in Virginia. My mother had just gone to her sister's house, she said with a long sigh, and found her dead.

I could tell by my mother's voice that she was in shock. I also knew she had more calls to make, as I have five siblings, and she would have to call each one of us to deliver the news. I wondered whom she had called first, thinking it was probably Sam, the eldest. She likely made the calls according to the order of our births; the elder children had known Posy longer than the others. There are six of us.

My studio at the colony was about one-third the size of Posy's bedroom, out of which she was at that moment being carried. Posy had a large bedroom, so there was enough space for me to pace around in as I called Stefanie, my wife, who was then my fiancé, to tell her the news. With me in the room were a metal desk, a twin bed, a bookshelf laden with the complete works of Shakespeare, and a bottle of bourbon I had brought from home. Drinking it felt, somehow, like the right thing to do, as if in light of the crisis I had a mandate to drink heavily. In a room that now felt as alien as it was, I filled my body with more liquor than it had contained in one night in years.

It was a long night. I stayed up late, watching films online of Cat Stevens and Paul Simon. There was no significance to these men and their songs; they had no connection to Posy that I knew of. But I was all alone, so I watched them, mesmerized, clinging to the Internet for solace at the pitch-dark, frozen colony.

The next morning, the pores of my skin were like the pores of a sponge that has been used to clean spilled whiskey off the floor of someone's bedroom. I had to go home. I had to call a car rental agency. The artists' colony was out in the country, so a rental agent had to drive out there and return me to it. Sitting beside him, I knew that if I could smell booze on me he could smell it too. But despite my smell and what it might have suggested about me—that I was a drunk person—he let me rent a little white Ford and take it north to Wheeling, West Virginia, where I grew up, where my parents still lived, and where Posy had spent the last few years of her life.

Thanksgiving was two days ahead, so as I barreled up the interstate I was surrounded all the way by holiday pilgrims. I imagined they were not unlike me, except they were probably on their way to see people who had survived the previous day, they were not coming from remote artists' colonies in rural settings, and they had not spent the last few days surrounded by a combination of painters, cows, and writers.

I arrived to find that the front steps at my parents' house were wet. It had not been raining. I soon learned that minutes before my arrival someone had walked outside and vomited wine all over the porch, then doused it with a bucket of soapy water.

As soon as I stepped into the house, all five of the dogs who had arrived before me—nearly 300 pounds of canine flesh—rushed the door, to bark at me and occupy the front entrance. A Newfoundland, a Great Dane, a Rat Terrier, a mutt, and a Pug, three of whom had traveled there with my siblings, two of whom lived with my parents, stampeded, preventing my advance into the house where I grew up. I pushed past the animals, but before I got five feet in, my sister-in-law Winnie and my sister Anne, both of whom had been drinking an awful lot of wine, one of whom was responsible for the condition of the steps, took turns embracing me. Before I had set my bags on the floor, they were telling me the story of the discovery of Posy's body.

~

My mother had gone looking for her sister after a week of not hearing from her.

Although they lived just two blocks from each other, Posy's silence was not unusual. She would often withdraw and insist on being alone for days at a time. She wouldn't answer her phone, or come to the door. It was, my mother said, a fine example of the kind of behavior she'd come to expect from her since they were children.

But it usually didn't last more than a few days at a time, and so after the third night of telephone silence my mother began walking to Posy's house. She went nightly, and didn't disturb Posy's isolation, but instead treaded the perimeter, to see if the lights were on, to look for evidence that someone inside was animate. Each night, the television glowed across the master bedroom, as if to reassure my mother that Posy dozed, still alive, before the History Channel.

When enough time passed without word from inside, my mother called the police.

Two officers escorted her through the front door, where she called Posy's name.

She called it again upon finding her sister absent from the living room, where on similar nights she had found her passed out on the couch.

Up the stairs she went with the cops, until they found my aunt in bed, the TV shining blue across her prostrate body. Posy faced the window that overlooked her garden, her head on a pillow. My mother called to her twice more, before one of the armed men pulled her aside and the other, seeing my aunt's flesh more closely, began calling in a

D.O.A.

Soon it was determined that Posy had been lying there, dead, for five days, based on her long silence—which had been sorely misread—and the condition of her corpse.

~

By the time I arrived in Wheeling, Posy's corpse was on its way to cremation. I would not see her again, live or dead—something I reminded myself of, over and over, but wanted not to accept. I knew she was gone, of course—my family is not one for cruel practical jokes—but some unthinking part of me was convinced I would find her in her living room, if I only walked over to see her there, as I had so many times before.

I understood, as I never had prior to this, why other people have open-casket funerals for their loved ones. I didn't want to have one for Posy. Neither did anyone else. But because I didn't see her body, there was no established point of transition between her life and her death.

It was as if she'd vanished suddenly; one moment she was alive in her home, and a moment later there was only her home, with the enormous sum of its contents, which would have to be reckoned with soon.

~

Posy's house was a tomb, now, filled with things once treasured by a woman whose absence from it was immanent. Prior to her death, a chair in her house may have had no one in it, but now it truly held no one; now it was brimming with vacancy, haunted by the empty air.

In the first days of her absence there, my five siblings and I faced a defunct home laden with the remains of a private life of fifty-nine years—diaries, photographs, art projects trapped forever in stages of incompletion, and literal tons of sundry other things. Every ounce was ours to inherit or discard. We had our work cut out for us. For legal reasons I didn't quite understand, though, we weren't supposed to touch anything, and had to wait a while before we started excavating.

We could not yet dismantle her house, but that didn't stop us from congregating in it. We would gather in her living room, in her kitchen, marveling at the mess she left behind.

It was Thanksgiving, in Posy's kitchen, which was no longer her kitchen, when the subject of inheritance first arose among members of my family. Posy had not had children, and had long since divorced her only husband, and so, when she drew up her will in her mid-fifties, she named as beneficiaries her six nephews and one niece—I, my sister and four brothers, and our lone cousin, who lives in Florida. There in the kitchen, my brother Jim asked our mother how much money she thought we stood to receive from our aunt's estate.

She didn't have an exact figure, but she speculated on some, listing Posy's retirement fund, her investments, and some trusts. I must have made a face, or something, because she pointed at me and said, smiling, "If it had been me instead of her, she would be sitting up in her room right now with an adding machine."

What my mother didn't know was that when I first learned Posy was dead, that night at the colony, as death's first shockwave began to wear off, at around three in the morning, I too had a moment at which I would have seized an adding machine, had the colony provided me one.

I knew that I had been named in Posy's will; she had told me so several times. She had never had a lucrative job, but I knew that some of my ancestors had made serious money and left it to their descendants. As evidence of this, when Posy moved to Wheeling she bought her sizable house outright—no mortgage necessary. If nothing else, I knew, I would at least inherit part of the house. I wouldn't get a million dollars, or half as much, or a fifth, but I knew I stood to benefit from her death. And so, for a minute in Virginia, I could not keep the grin from my drunken face.

~

No one who was qualified to would sign Posy's death certificate. My mother had to ask a state official to pressure Posy's ex-doctor to do it. The holidays were on, and everyone, it seemed, had something else to do.

Then we had Thanksgiving dinner, and for days the clergyman

was booked. We had to work around his schedule.

I waited as long as I felt I could for Posy's burial, but eventually I thought I should return to the artists' colony. I had two weeks left to spend there, with a studio, private room and no obligations, not even to cook. I didn't even have to write if I didn't want to.

I thought it would be ungrateful of me not to return. Nothing in Wheeling was likely to change; Posy would not be getting any more or less dead.

My mother agreed that I should go. She insisted that the funeral was not so important, that Posy would be cremated, given the quickest of graveside services, and installed beside or inside an exclusive, private mausoleum, centrally located at Wheeling's Greenwood Cemetery.

I learned, when discussing this with my brother Sam, that several of our maternal cousins are on the board at Greenwood Cemetery. He thought I should have already known that. But it never occurred to me to ask about this, in all my life; I'd always felt safe enough in assuming that no cemeteries were owned by my cousins.

~

I left, then, and back at the colony I tried to continue some writing projects that appeared, in light of recent events, trivial. Even my friend Jerry, whom I had been writing about in my first few colony days, seemed a distant concern.

Not one month before Posy left this world, Jerry died of a heroin overdose. Like me and Posy, he grew up in Wheeling; like Posy, his life ended there.

From a distance, physically speaking, Jerry and I were nearly identical—same height, same shoulders, similar faces—but in other ways we could not have been more different. As a teenager, I spent most of my time indoors, impatiently waiting out my adolescence. Jerry, I heard, spent this simultaneous phase of his life (we were born days apart in the same city, possibly the same hospital) selling LSD, making money, and eventually getting caught by his father and put on an informal house arrest for what I understand was a very long time.

Jerry was a painter—a talented one who dropped out of art

school in his early twenties when he broke his arm skateboarding and couldn't paint for a month.

He would drink heavily and ask close friends to punch him as hard as they could in the face. If they declined, he might pick a fight with a stranger, then refuse to defend himself when the swinging started. It wasn't an art project.

In the middle of his twenties, Jerry attempted suicide. When paramedics came to his rescue he leapt out the back of their moving ambulance, to be discovered, minutes later, unconscious among some trees.

In his final year of life, after a fistfight, his jaw had to be wired shut. Annoyed with the wires, he got drunk and removed them with pliers and some other tools.

Jerry was a generator of harrowing anecdotes, but I found, ultimately, that there was not much more I could say about him than to retell these stories that provided anything but a complete picture of their subject. I had known Jerry, and in a way I'd admired him, but I couldn't do him justice in writing. My effort to describe his life stalled.

Jerry, for that matter, had been a distraction from my book project. I had gone to the colony in order to write about inanimate things. I had once written with great enthusiasm, and with some success, about my great-grandfather's walking stick. I had also written about a wooden club, and had written another essay about a bag of dirty laundry that was left in my old apartment in Ohio by a German woman. I was asked many times at the colony what I was writing, and I explained as many times, to different listeners, that my plan was to write a collection of short pieces about inanimate things. They would come together as a book, I said, one that I hoped would be worth reading. Every time I described it, I was less convinced of the likelihood of this.

My secret anxiety was that I had run out of objects worth writing about. I couldn't just run to the nearest department store and purchase a laundry basket, so that it could be the subject of my next contemplative prose piece.

Now, though, I was about to take on more objects than I could possibly write about in one book, all of them pregnant with meaning to someone who was now gone.

Alone at the colony, drinking coffee that I took from Posy's house, I started to write about some of those objects, and more particularly about the woman who, until just days before, had called them her own.

~

Posy was born in 1950 and grew up in Wheeling, in a big house about half a mile from the one I was raised in, which is two blocks away from the one where she died. At twenty-one, she married a man who looks, in photographs from the wedding, like a failed attempt at cloning Steve Stills. They lived together in England a few years, and then moved into a townhouse in a suburb of Washington, D.C. In the early Eighties they divorced, but Posy remained at the townhouse, with a cherry tree in the front yard and, eventually, a peeping tom across the backyard, whom she referred to for years after he moved in as "Mr. Peepers."

When I met Posy for the first time, I didn't realize what an enormous presence she would have in my life. I didn't even know that I had hands yet; I had just been born. But as I grew older, and as Posy came, on occasion, to visit us in Wheeling from out of town, my fascination with my aunt grew.

I used to watch Posy put on makeup. It is my earliest memory of her, and one of my first vivid memories. Each morning, when she stayed with us, I would sit on a twin bed and lose myself in her beautification. Before she applied rouge, she announced that she would apply rouge. I would stare, fascinated, three or four years old.

As I grew older, I learned that in addition to wearing makeup Posy drank. My brother David used to complain that our aunt would call his house in the middle of the night, drunk and wanting to talk; when I made it to college, my phone rang often at similar hours and for the same reason: the need to speak to someone had overtaken my aunt during one of her binges, and she knew that if I picked up the phone I would stay on the line as long as she wanted.

Aside from these interminable calls, Posy kept her habit from everyone, as if it were a secret, confining it to her private life until the very end. She never drank in front of members of our family, as far as I know, and when I knew her as an adult, she referred to her "drinking days" as if they were far behind her.

110

~

I was seventeen when I started making periodic visits to Posy in D.C. Shortly before my first trip, I complained to my mother how bored I'd become. I was living at home, in a town I didn't like. I was not resourceful enough to take matters into my own hands and flee to a better place, like Pittsburgh, or Columbus, Ohio.

My mother said, "Go visit your aunt Posy."

A couple of phone calls and a day later, I was on a bus.

Eight hours into the eight-hour trip, just as I'd been getting used to the bus, I found myself standing on the asphalt outside the station with an aunt I could hardly remember. She pulled me into an embrace. She spoke to me as if she knew me very well.

She did, it turns out—only she had gotten to know me at an age when I was bound to forget how well acquainted we were. She had not visited Wheeling in years; I hadn't seen her.

In her house, after she died, I found a box that contained a tall stack of photos of us, together. We are sitting at a table, or standing by a tree. In most of them I am no older than five. I don't know who took them—probably my mother.

The memorable times we had when I was a child—of which there were evidently many—are mere photographs to me, despite the faded images in my head of her arriving to my parents' home after a long drive and bending down to say hello to me, the joints of her legs creaking and snapping like the branches of an ancient tree.

Although I had known her distantly all my life, it was in D.C., as a teenager, that I first learned what a curious, inquisitive person my aunt was. Perpetually interested in everything, she knew the names of species of birds, flowers, and trees. She could write in hieroglyphics. She could, it seemed, be fascinated by any minute idiosyncrasy of the world, naturally occurring or manufactured. She would zero in on them one at a time, as we took long walks beside lakes and went to museums.

I would repeat the voyage to see her in years to follow, and in the course of them I learned a precious array of tricks useful only on buses. I gathered from observation that sitting by the window and pretending to be asleep with your luggage piled on the seat beside you is a foolproof, heartless way to avoid sitting next to a stranger.

I took friends and girlfriends with me to see Posy. She once asked me and then-girlfriend Valerie, "If for the rest of your life you could eat only one type of grain, what would you choose?" She was on the edge of her seat, literally, in anticipation of our responses. I chose rice, forgetting that bread was a form of grain. Posy chose bread.

We went to museums, international food stores, and historic districts of small cities in Virginia. On weekend afternoons, in pricey supermarkets, we "grazed"—that is, ate all of the free samples we could without actually buying anything.

I did not know, as we did this, that Posy was in fact very wealthy. We could have bought all of the food that she insisted we eat in small portions for free. We could have bought a small grocery store.

In the early evenings, we would walk through her Virginian suburb as she pointed with great disgust to the houses where, she declared, she thought very seriously of sticking post-it notes on the doors, to critique her neighbors' decorations, and decisions with regard to paint color. It was one of her unrealized ambitions, to apply these notes all over town and become an anonymous house critic.

One July afternoon in historic Alexandria, Virginia, we passed a woman decked head to toe in clothing made of prints of the American flag. Posy waited until she was out of earshot to turn to my brother Jim and me to say, in an affected old-money tone, "I regret to say that I neglected to bring my post-its to Alexandria."

Posy cooked, but rarely ate. I didn't find this significant. I was used to it, in fact, as I grew up with a mother who cooked for her family but never sat down to a meal. When Posy prepared elaborate dishes involving fish and vegetables, but didn't touch them afterward, I didn't find it odd.

I recall the fish in particular because I didn't eat it either. I was always reluctant to eat Posy's food because I didn't want to take anything away from her. I didn't want to be a burden on her, or a consumer of her things. I thought she would probably want to eat the fish—it looked delicious, face still attached, on its bed of rice—and I didn't want to prevent her from enjoying it by devouring it first. I was the kind of young man who approached a buffet as he would a tightrope; I had always to balance my need for sustenance against my reluctance to take so much food that someone else would go without something he wanted, like corn pudding. So I didn't touch the fish Posy had made, when she left it out for me one night. Neither did she. She could have told me she would like me to eat it; I could have asked her if I was supposed to. Neither of us said a word about it. She preserved it in the refrigerator, and a few days later I saw the whole uneaten fish, showered with its rice, looking up at me from the bottom of the trashcan.

Posy would go to bed early every night; I would go out, restless, and wander the antiseptic slice of Virginia in which she spent most of her life. When I got to be old enough to drink legally—a time when my visits grew less frequent, as I had developed what was starting to resemble a life of my own—I would wander a mile to the nearest supermarket, on foot, and return to Posy's with a couple of large bottles of Miller High Life hanging from my hand in a plastic bag. I'd drink them down and throw them out as Posy slept, tossing the bottles in her garbage can, where I now realize she must have found them in the morning.

I was oblivious, mostly, to Posy's struggle against her appetite for booze. The desperation of it was beyond me, anyway. She never talked about it, so if she minded that her young nephew was drinking alone at night in her home and leaving bottles for her to find, I didn't know it. As in the case of the wasted fish, I am left to wonder now if any of this left the impression on her it did on me.

~

The longest visit I ever made to Posy was in the summer of my twenty-third year. I had gone to San Francisco for a couple of weeks, to visit a friend and shake off a breakup that had hollowed me out. I tried (much-belatedly) to smoke pot for the first time, drank enough coffee to float a ship, and wandered the city's streets as frantically as if I were searching for something.

I stayed long enough to wear out my welcome, then bought a plane ticket for D.C., where I knew I could take refuge in a home that was familiar to me.

I spent three weeks at Posy's, doing next to nothing. I lounged at the community's pool; I got sunburnt; we watched television; we took day trips to parks, where we walked and Posy provided what all of San

Francisco couldn't give: love of the blood relative variety, and all of its attendant patience.

I know, now, that Posy must have been frustrated with me. I had come screaming in from California with no clue what to do with myself. I thought I might not return to Ohio, where I'd been living and attending more school. I was lost in the way that young people without children or mortgages have the luxury of being lost, at an age that makes one's elders scratch their heads, when decisions seem not nearly as momentous to oneself as they do to others, who know that time and idle youth are precious.

I know why I went to Posy, though, and no one else. I needed to be with a born listener. Always eager to hear what someone had to say, she would drop everything in order to have a conversation, no matter what about. Some families are populated with these types exclusively; ours had only one.

~

Most of the talking and listening I did with Posy was done on the phone. She would spend a day drinking, and calling friends and relatives. I learned to determine, when she called, whether or not she was sober, by the way she did or did not slur certain words. When she was drunk, she would speak emphatically about everything, then forget our conversation soon after we had it. I learned not to refer to our most recent interactions, for fear of embarrassing both of us.

Usually, though, she wasn't drunk, and sometime before she moved to Wheeling, when her death was hardly in sight, we spoke by phone about Randall Jarrell's poem "The Death of the Ball Turret Gunner." I don't recall what prompted the conversation. Its context is lost to forgetfulness, but I recall distinctly what it was we said. I suspect that Posy had just gone to an air show and seen a bomber with a ball turret, and been reminded of the poem—but possibly not; hers was a mind that wandered often, to what could appear to be unlikely places, to those of us with whom she shared her thoughts.

Neither I nor Posy knew who wrote the poem (I wrongly suggested Keith Douglas), but she knew its final line by heart: "When I died they washed me out of the turret with a hose."

Of course she remembered it: she was always preoccupied by death, whether it be her mother's, her father's, her own, or someone else's. And she was thoroughly taken with the gallantry that attends a wartime casualty, even if Jarrell gives his gunner a fate that is anything but glorious.

In keeping with Posy's military fascination, whenever I went to see her in D.C., as a teenager and in my early twenties, she never failed to take me to a particular Army-Navy surplus shop in Alexandria, Virginia. Some of my fondest memories of time spent with her are set among rucksacks and empty service pistols.

On one visit, Posy and I found at the surplus shop replica vodka flasks from the KGB—roundish, steel containers with little spouts for pouring vodka into Russian mouths, and images of Lenin's head on their removable caps. Smitten with them, we each bought one. When I mentioned it later to my brother David, he pointed out that for me the flask was a funny novelty item, but our aunt would likely put hers to use.

I didn't think he was serious then, and today I think he was wrong. Posy was the kind of drinker who kept her habit at home. She would shut herself in and drink for a weekend, or for the duration of her retirement, rather than move about the outside world intoxicated. She didn't need a flask for that.

Now Posy's novelty flask is mine, which makes sense, as between the two of us I am the one who still drinks. I keep it in my kitchen cupboard, next to my thermos and French press.

~

In 2004, still living in D.C., Posy had a massive heart attack that technically killed her for several minutes. Paramedics managed to revive her. It spooked her enough that she moved to Wheeling, the city of her birth and future death. The reason for her move was that there my mother could look after her, but now that I know her fate I am reminded of the elephant's supposed tendency to travel many miles to his graveyard in order to die.

In Wheeling, she found and bought the house that would hold her massive wardrobe, inherited furniture, and enormous collection of miscellaneous things. With three spacious bedrooms, two living rooms, a dining room, a kitchen, and an ample basement with what once was a servant's quarters, the house was too big for one person. It stood at some remove from a busy road with a row of tall, thick bushes to provide it cover. On one side was another house. On the other was a generous yard with gardens full of flowers I lack the floral diction to describe. Posy told me their names, but I forgot them.

~

Several weeks after Posy died, when I'd returned from the colony, I received a letter in Missouri that began with a sentence of nearly one-hundred words. It read,

> The persons or organizations listed below are hereby notified that on the 1st day of December 2009, document dated the 5th day of December 2008, purporting to be the Last Will and Testament of Rose McKennan H_____, who died on November 23, 2009, were delivered to the undersigned Clerk of the County Commission of Ohio County, West Virginia, for safe keeping in her office until proceedings may be had for the probate thereof, or until it is demanded by an Executor or other person authorized to demand it, for the purpose of having it proved according to law.

The letter containing this brick of a sentence accompanied a copy of Posy's will, which was like the letter in its density. Through the document, Posy did the sort of thing one does in a will: named my eldest brother Sam as executor, and ordered him to sell her house and distribute her estate equally to nephews and niece.

Having spent much of my life writing and reading things like essays, poems and novels, I never imagined, though it seems inevitable in hindsight, that the document with the greatest influence on my life—at least materially—would be one composed under Posy's consultation by a couple of lawyers.

A last will and testament is the only means I know of for a corpse to influence its survivors, outside of scenes depicted in horror movies. A will can decide the fortunes of living persons, bestowing on them swords, bookshelves and money. It can also decide how a family will spend its time together over the holidays.

Posy's will returned me to Wheeling that Christmas, where we would have another holiday without Posy and take the next step in the process of inheritance. Our aunt's property had to be doled out among us, and so six of her will's beneficiaries—our late uncle's son couldn't make the trip from Florida—met at her house. Each of us, separately, went from kitchen to living room to sitting room to foyer to sun room to downstairs spare bedroom, then upstairs to the multiple rooms there, cataloguing what we did and did not want. We who were still alive made lists, on legal pads, of what we would soon call our own.

Everyone in my family had feelings about this process of claiming Posy's things. Mostly we maintained an appearance of indifference. I tried to behave as if the process were a burden worth shouldering on behalf of Posy, who must have expected us to go about things as we did. But the sorting of Posy's things seemed rushed to me, the effort to disperse them unreasonably urgent. Posy had spent nearly sixty years accruing her domestic cargo; we would parcel it out in a day. I would have felt no differently about this had I broken into her house as she slept and taken what I could before she woke.

Her house was in a state of what it would be generous to call disarray. The kitchen counter was piled with old mail, plants, books, and half-finished bottles of water and medicine. Littering the floor of a walk-in closet were spools of yarn, batches of paper, vinyl records and a hundred other things.

My brother Sam decreed that one of us had to take pictures of every room, to record the condition of Posy's home and document the things she had owned. I volunteered.

I still have the photos, which offer glimpses of the last stage of Posy's life—of her things as she preferred them to be unto the night of her death, and as they remained until we swept them into boxes.

In the hallway stands a glass case from the office of her father's medical practice, displaying miscellanea like railroad spikes and antique spoons. Atop the case is an alarm clock made from the talking model of a B-17; above it hangs a severed, taxidermied deer's head. In the fireplace of the living room where I often sat with Posy is a World War I artillery shell that was converted to a lamp, a cement cat who holds binoculars to his eyes, and an old vase from somewhere overseas, bought by a couple of our ancestors. In a photo of the corner of Posy's living room, a grandfather clock stands handsome but broken, useless for keeping time. In her front hallway, on a table, sits the bust of a woman whose face is obscured by a shroud.

From the kitchen ceiling fan hangs Turbofrog, a frog made of papier-mâché out of whose rear protrude a pair of smoking tailpipes. Posy made him in D.C. and mentioned him every time we spoke on the phone for a year. He accompanied her to Wheeling, so in one photo he hangs from a fan blade, suspended in air, his tongue lolling.

~

Posy's big house was filled with stuff, and most of it was, to us, so much stuffing, with some exceptions. Two coveted items were swords—the one I would take, plus another one of similar look and origin.

Another hot thing was a pair of wooden chairs from the dining room, which I ultimately let my sister have in exchange for a couple of small paintings by a local artist who is missing an arm. The only things I know about him are that he paints and has only one arm.

My inheritance list was short. On it was the bookshelf in Posy's upstairs guest room that featured windowpanes for looking in and seeing the books. I listed the child's dresser Posy kept in a corner of her big bedroom, as Stefanie and I were planning to have a child someday who might use it. I listed a rocking chair in which I had been rocked as a baby, which my mother and Posy had been rocked in as well. I had no children at the time, but I had them in mind when I noted on paper my desire for these things.

I also thought, as I made my list, that I would somehow have to earn every ounce of the combined weight of all the things on it. If I was to inherit money, which seemed likely, I would have to prove myself worthy of it somehow.

Of course I didn't really have to do that. It is not how inheritance works. I wasn't getting paid for doing anything; I was getting paid for having been related to Posy.

Look: I didn't have the sense of entitlement that comes in handy when faced with an inheritance. I knew how fortunate I was to be faced with it at all, but my good fortune was unsettling. I had never had much money. I had never had nice furniture. Now this nicer furniture than I could afford was mine if I wanted it. It wouldn't cost anything. I couldn't help feeling, in a small way, like a criminal.

Someone knocked at the door. It was the end of list-making day. My brothers Jim and David and I stood in the front entrance to Posy's house, about to leave. Immediately I dreaded having to open it. I did not want to tell Posy's visitor she was not at home and never again would be.

David opened the door slowly. On the other side stood Cheryl.

A middle-aged woman with short, blonde hair and earrings the size of my ears, Cheryl spoke to us at a volume I found was unreasonably high, given the short distance between her and us. She knew already that Posy was dead. She was looking for my mother. As long as we were standing there, though, she said that the three of us were handsome.

She reassured us, then, that Posy, though dead, was in the house—that she was still with us, and was there to comfort us. David told her he would tell our mother she stopped by. On her way out, she said that spontaneous, effusive singing was the most effective way to combat grief.

It was not the first time I had ever met Cheryl.

A year and eleven months before her death, Posy abruptly stopped drinking—after months of bingeing—and had a seizure. The doctors induced a coma, to save her from her body's revolt at this sudden withdrawal, and so she spent that Christmas unconscious, on a respirator and feeding tube.

I went to see her in her hospital bed, but I hardly remember how she looked. I hardly looked at her. I recall distinctly my gut disbelief that it was her at all. Surely I am not the first to observe that someone on a respirator appears to be one incidental piece of the machines she is attached to—which, I had not known before then, are loud. I recall that we arrived at Posy's mealtime, as a white liquid coursed through one of the tubes that fed into her body.

My mother suggested I say hello, as she was certain that Posy could hear me; I, doubtful, tried this out, got as far as the first half of "Hi," and then turned away from the machines into the hallway where, standing next to Winnie with my hands over my face, a nurse confronted us to ask what we were doing.

She thought we didn't belong on the ward. She didn't realize there was a patient there.

Cheryl arrived, soon after that. When she found me, my mother and Winnie sitting at a small table down the hall from Posy, she swept into the room to interrupt. She introduced herself to me, and as she stood there she explained with great certainty what was going on. She insisted that despite the condition of Posy's body, her spirit was there in the room with us. Posy, she said, was listening to us that moment, keeping us company and wishing she could brighten the mood.

A firm believer in the limitations of the body, and in the gravity of a coma, I disagreed with Cheryl, but kept silent in deference to my mother, who listened politely.

The longer Cheryl remained, to say these things with the assurance of a false prophet, the more I wanted to put my hand over her mouth and back her out of the room.

"I was just upstairs with Randall," she said after a pause.

My mother looked stunned. She asked what Cheryl meant, and Cheryl said, "He's here." She pointed up. She didn't mean that he was a visiting, wandering spirit; he was on the ward above us. "As soon as he heard about Posy being in here," she said, "he had a heart attack!"

This information was not without its significance.

It is generally accepted, among members of my family, that Cheryl's friend Randall helped to accelerate the death of Posy.

Soon after she moved to Wheeling, Randall came to Posy's house to ask for work. She was planting flowers in her garden, and gave him some yard work to do. Soon he moved into the apartment above her garage. Then they started sleeping together.

Randall was a large Wheeling native, about 6'2" and built like a tall sack of mulch, with perpetually unkempt beard and glasses. He was just over forty but looked fifty-five. He had several children with different mothers, none of whom he was allowed to see because of the violence he inflicted on them, or so I understood. For years he had been killing himself slowly with vodka and cigarettes, to the chagrin of everyone who would have liked to see him take a quicker route.

There are lots of things I don't like to think about, and Randall is one of them.

He would spend a weekend or week at a time drinking on Posy's couch. He was not a passive drunk. He once shoved Posy down her basement stairs, a steep set of hard, wooden steps. For days after, she wandered her big house as drunk as Randall, bruised and bleeding into her hair, neglecting to clean the gash he had made across her head. On another day, in another month, he threw Posy across her kitchen, as she tried to call the police, to report whatever else he had been doing. I heard this from my mother, who heard it and things like it from Posy on those occasions when she tossed Randall out—often with the aid of police—and spent a few days without him, only to welcome him back again every time.

Because I lived five-hundred miles away, I was only vaguely aware of this abuse as it went on, but after Posy died my mother said it was a monthly—if not weekly—occurrence for Randall to be taken from Posy's house in handcuffs, for one reason or another. That Randall, with his record of domestic abuse inflicted on multiple women, harmed Posy physically, explained why, when I visited, her arms were often covered with bruises. She shrugged and said they were a side effect of her heart medicine.

I am one of the only members of my family who ever met Randall. I shook his hand once, early in his affair with Posy, perhaps before the abuse started, who knows.

A few of the times I came to see my aunt, Randall lounged drunk on a couch in another room as she and I sat together and talked, until he wandered in and stood there, hovering behind me in the doorway, not speaking. In a big living room that featured an array of unlikely ornaments—the statue of a samurai, a dragon head whose teeth were an exact replica of Posy's—Randall was my least favorite of them all.

On the same afternoon we made our lists at Posy's, Randall got drunk somewhere and made a series of unanswered phone calls to my parents' house. On his third attempt to reach my mother he left a message, listing for her the things still in the house that belonged to him: a Christmas ornament Posy had bought him when he asked for it, and a crate filled with records, which I had put on my inheritance list.

We agreed that Randall's claims were not legitimate, that whatever the house held when Posy died was now ours. We owed him nothing. At the end of his message, Randall added that Posy had loved him.

~

When my mother and I went to check on Posy's house one night, soon after Christmas, we heard, upon opening the door, a hideous banging noise that came from the rear of the building. It could have been the mechanical noise of pipes, as the heat was coming on; of course that was what it was, and we knew it. But although the house was empty of people and specters, my imagination filled it with all the macabre inventions it could produce in a half-second. My mother and I fled the house and circled it instead, peering through windows to reassure ourselves that Randall had not made his way inside, to do something foolish like bang on pipes.

Posy's house was one that could readily inspire fear, in part because any house old and large enough can scare people. Its layout didn't help. When you walked in, the first thing you faced was a wall, about ten feet ahead. On the other side was the kitchen, in which there could have been anything—a killer, a rabid animal, a drunk man hitting pipes with an object—so that to be greeted by the house with a repeated, anonymous clang could have meant anything. Posy's house was not designed with the comfort of nervous people in mind.

I was not afraid of Randall. I am strong enough to do harm with blunt instruments, and usually sober. Randall was much older, out of shape, and usually drunk. I could have split his head like a cantaloupe if I had something solid to hit him with.

In fact, Posy had a monstrous executioner's sword on display in her house, plus a couple of sabers, any one of which I could have put to use against Randall, to end its era of dormancy and his era of activity.

For these reasons, I wasn't really afraid of Randall; rather, it was my mother's fear of Randall, of the very possibility of having to confront him, that unnerved me. Her anxieties are contagious. Whenever I went to Posy's house, I could feel him looming on the ends of my nerves, though I knew he must have been downing vodka on the other side of town.

On another, later morning, my mother and I were at Posy's house again when Cheryl arrived, once again. My mother let her in. After some idle talk concerning Posy's afterlife experience, as I sat playing with a letter opener, Cheryl reminded us that Randall still felt certain he had some things coming to him. My mother said, politely, that she wouldn't hand them over. Cheryl said, "Anne, all you have to say is, 'They're already gone,' if that's what you want. All you have to do is say it." After a long sigh, my mother said it, and Cheryl stayed for twenty minutes more, to talk about the house and Posy's things.

She insisted to us that "a broken heart" had killed my aunt, and her reason for thinking so was this: the last time Randall left rehab, when Posy was still living, he emerged to tell her he had met someone else—another woman—while inside. This happened two weeks before Posy's death.

After she died, used tissues were found strewn about her house, the crying spells that prompted them the result, presumably, of Randall's cold, bad news.

I announced that we had work to do, and my mother, irrepressibly polite, ushered Cheryl slowly out the door. When we were finally alone, my mother said that whenever she went to Posy's house Cheryl would arrive as if on cue. We had to start parking somewhere else and walking to Posy's, so that Cheryl wouldn't drive past, see the car outside, and come knocking.

~

Cheryl—metaphysical Cheryl—had raised an essential question.

Something had killed my aunt. She had drunk herself to death, it was clear enough. But there was more to her slow self-destruction than that.

Randall had probably broken her heart, as Cheryl said, but I knew that Posy had been through worse breakups with better men and come out of them alive. Her trouble ran more deeply than Cheryl knew.

Posy had spent most of her last several years locked up in her house, willfully alone. I could not say why that was, but now I found that I wanted to. I did not want Cheryl to have the last word, to decide for herself or for anyone what it was that had ended my dear aunt's life.

I was starting to see that there was something it was up to me to do; that perhaps I ought to try to make sense of the wreck that Posy left behind when she died.

For the time being, though, there was other work to do.

~

Two days after Christmas, a team of us converged on Posy's house with cups of coffee from a gas station in hand, determined to penetrate the layers of dust and lingering reek of cigarette smoke. We had made and negotiated our lists; now it was time to make the place look as if Posy hadn't lived there.

We had done some of this already, at Thanksgiving, when my brother David and I disposed of the mattress on which our aunt had died.

It was clear which side she had expired on. Roughly a third of it was deeply stained with a brown that verged on red and spilled in what must have been a pool across the fabric.

We were silent as we flipped the mattress upright and carried it across the bedroom, into the hallway, and down the narrow steps. I said, "Let's not take this through the kitchen. Let's go out the front door." He nodded; our mother was in the kitchen, with a couple of siblings. Even if they had seen it already, I thought we should spare them the appearance of this deathbed.

We dragged it out to the alley, for the garbage truck to take when it came. Doing the most morbid work I had ever done, I told myself that I was, at that moment, earning every cent I would get from Posy's estate. I didn't really believe it.

We cleared out of the house everything that wasn't of value to us or to the man who would soon auction whatever we didn't want. Food, medicine, refrigerator magnets, dental floss, toilet brushes, condiments, and bags of generic tea all had to be tossed. We emptied the cupboards and packed everything that couldn't be used or reused into a crate or paper bag. We filled the front hallway with it, where a whole domestic life, replete with herbs and toothpaste, sat ready for ejection.

When I returned, later, to my parents' house, two blocks away, I couldn't help estimating how many grocery bags it would take to haul off all the pills in their medicine cabinet—one, I guessed. I looked in their freezer and pictured myself emptying their ice cream and cold meat into a trashcan.

At the end of our first day spent cleaning at Posy's, David told our mother, "Before you die, sell everything."

No one had told this to Posy, and if someone had I know she would have ignored him, based on how much of her house was occupied by an assortment of things I have come to euphemize by calling it "miscellany." By this I mean watering cans, brooms, statuettes, peacock feathers, and metal stands meant to hold lord-knows-what. This does not even begin to catalogue Posy's belongings, none of which were where they should have been, if most of them could have been said to belong anywhere.

The most baffling thing of all was left sitting on the coffee table in Posy's living room. It was a paper plate, placed conspicuously at the room's center, and on its back was written a contract. In penciled scribble it read,

I anm [sic] not
responsible for
any accident that may
happen to me *or my property*

Below this was Posy's signature, below it her address, and below that the signature of Randall.

None of us knew exactly what to make of it. Certainly it was not a legally binding contract, but none could say with certainty whether Randall would have known that, or whether Posy realized it, in whatever state she was in when it was written. I hoped it was drawn up in jest, but it was more likely scribbled out of Randall's worry that he would be held accountable for whatever harm he might bring her next.

My mother, who was convinced in those days that Randall had murdered her sister, thought this plate must have had something to do with the chain of events that led him to kill her. It must have been part of an ill-conceived plan, she thought, that entailed the death of the only other remaining member of the family she grew up in.

Others among us, while they did not necessarily connect it with a specific crime, saw it as evidence that Randall had at the very least had bad intentions.

The only clear evidence I saw in it was of the sort of company my aunt kept in her retirement.

~

Ours was a repeat performance, of a drama that has been staged in countless homes in the wakes of countless deaths.

Several are the poets who have described that drama in their poems.

When she died, Anne Sexton's mother shouldered her with the same blessing Posy left me: one great fraction of her estate. "The Division of Parts" is the poem Sexton produced in response to this generous encumbrance. It begins with the arrival in the mail of her mother's will. "This is the division of money," she writes in response to it. "I am one third / of your daughters counting my bounty." Sexton is doing something a poem allows for, which is to address the person, now dead, who generated her inheritance. She has been given a portion of her mother's things, and—in a way—many pieces of her mother. The poem goes on, Sexton listing her mother's old clothes, among them "the gaudy fur animals / I do not know how to use," which, she says, "settle on me like a debt."

That she calls this a debt, and portrays herself as the debtor, points out exactly the problem with inheritance I found myself facing in Wheeling. It is the fate of the conscientious inheritor, to feel as if she owes more than gratitude to the one who generated her sudden fortune, even if the fortune is modest and its transmission ordained by a notarized document.

A gift given at the precise moment when someone ceases to be is one that cannot be answered. There can be no expression of gratitude; one cannot send a thank-you note to a grave site. One cannot express anything to the dead, which is part of what makes Sexton's poem, and others like it, heartbreaking. They are often addressed to the dead giver of gifts, but of course they are read by strangers, like me, so that they are performances of failures to communicate at the same time that they do, in fact, communicate something.

~

When Posy made her move from D.C. to Wheeling, years before her death, those who helped her urged her to get rid of things, to make her cargo lighter for the trip. There was a tremendous lot of stuff she did not need; they couldn't imagine what she would do with all of the things she had.

As it turned out, as they suspected, with most of them she did nothing. For the years they spent with her in Wheeling, her possessions languished in the same state in which they had traveled.

We discovered unopened cardboard boxes on every floor of Posy's home—boxes that had been packed for her move to Wheeling. They came in all sizes and held all manner of stuff. Tall boxes with metal rods stuck into their ceilings had Posy's clothes hanging in them. There were nearly a dozen of them, huge and full. This was in addition to what Posy had bothered to take out of the boxes to fill her closets.

When she was nineteen, I would later find, she wrote in her diary, "I want to live in a fantasy world of clothes." It appeared as if she had spent her adult life trying to live out that fantasy.

I did not want to have these things.

I have only twice in my life put on articles of women's clothing. Once was at a party in high school; it was a favor for a friend who was moving away, and I got nothing out of the experience, except that I thought I looked better in my friend's dress than she did; it showed off the muscles of my chest.

No one else in the family wanted Posy's clothes, despite the readiness with which they, and I, took so many of her other belongings. Clothing has a way of retaining more of its previous owner than any other type of possession does, I suspect, if only because of its contact with its owner's body. If anything is to carry its owner's smell, it is bound to be a pair of socks or pants. Therefore, whereas my little brother had no problem seizing Posy's dishes, neither my mother, my sister, Winnie, nor Stefanie wanted Posy's clothes—not even the garments with tags still attached. It wasn't just because Posy was smaller than these people. It was because wearing a dead woman's clothes could and perhaps would seem to be a violation, as if wearing Posy's clothes would be like putting on her skin.

Since no one wanted the contents of Posy's closets, in the days of this liquidation I drove them in several trips to the local Goodwill. There they would still be the contents of a dead woman's wardrobe, but they would hang from racks with new price tags, sufficiently divorced from any evidence of her.

Some of her clothes we had to throw away. There was a home-made pirate outfit, deep in one of her cavernous wardrobes, and it seemed doubtful that anyone in our landlocked city would want one of those.

~

In "A Woman Mourned by Daughters," Adrienne Rich lingers in the house of her mother, writing, "we sit here in your kitchen, / spent, you see, already." Like Sexton, she addresses her mother directly, but she is in another room, "puffed up in death / like a corpse pulled from the sea."

But the body will not sit still. It grows until it permeates the scene completely. "You are swollen," she writes, "till you strain / this house and the whole sky." Then, with a certain sleight-of-hand, Rich locates her mother elsewhere in the house, manifested in the things that were once hers. "You breathe upon us now," she writes, "through solid assertions / of yourself"—and among these are "teaspoons," "a forest / of old plants," and "an old man in an adjoining / room to be touched and fed." The mother's body becomes the things that surround it, as it lies there. The mother becomes everything, in the literal sense that several members of my family could be found in the same room, as she inhabits the multiplied obligations that her death made possible. Rich tells her mother, on behalf of herself and her sisters, "we groan beneath your weight."

~

There were moments when the cleanup effort brought us together, in the literal sense that several could be found in the same room for an hour at a time. Three or four would gather and sort old magazines, or throw out other things we knew no one would want. Even my father was present for some of this, despite his general preference to stay out of everyone's way.

Stefanie, who had flown in to join me and help us out at Posy's, distinguished herself by collecting Posy's shoes in a crate so that they could be removed from the premises efficiently. In response, my mother—who was given, in those days of fresh grief, to dramatic gestures—shouted to the emptying house her approval for her daughter-in-law-to-be. "Oh, Stefanie," she cried so that everyone could hear. "We are keeping her!"

Under my mother's direction, I stood before Posy's dresser and threw handfuls of her nightgowns and underwear into a garbage bag. Halfway through the job, I reached in among some more fabrics and felt what I immediately knew was not an article of clothing but a vibrator. What else, I thought, would be hard yet fleshy in an underwear drawer?

As soon as I had it in my grasp I let it go. I didn't want to be the one to pull the dead woman's sex toy from her bureau, so I abandoned my post and walked to the other side of the room. My mother took over.

Immediately, she pulled the phallus out of the drawer and looked at it. She blinked. I watched, glad to be old enough that I would probably not develop a new neurosis from the sight of this. After a long pause, my mother jumped and said, "Oh! Oh my god! Posy!" And she threw the dildo back into the drawer, laughing with disbelief. She made a joke about how clueless she is with such things. She declared that Posy must be very proud of herself.

I had wanted someone else to find the vibrator and discreetly throw it in the trash, but as it happened I had to wrap it in a nightgown and stuff it in the bag myself. My sister asked if it had a vibration feature, and Winnie said, "Oh, I think they all do now, pretty much."

I didn't know if she was right about that. I didn't want to argue.

After the worthless and genitally-oriented things were gone from Posy's, we had to move on to the things whose worth was less questionable, my aunt's papers first among them. Of these there were many boxes' worth in the basement, plus a couple of filing cabinets.

A manila envelope held Posy's divorce papers, which seemed to be worth keeping, or probably were for a few years after 1982. I couldn't say the same for the envelope stuffed with phone bills from 1980, or the bank documents that spanned the course of her marriage. We kept all of Posy's tax returns, but nearly everything else we destroyed. I disposed of hundreds of files that held papers from banks and utilities, plus maintenance records for cars she hadn't owned in decades.

I shredded Posy's old medical bills. My grandfather's Civil War historian club membership card, which Posy had kept in a box, went through the machine, and so did still more receipts from 1992, 1972, and every year in between, plus more. As I fed them in I wondered what she would have said, had she somehow been there to accompany me. It might have been something very funny.

Sifting through the formal drivel, I came across a notebook with three loose pages stuck in back.

On them was Posy's account of a long, lucidly recalled dream in which she behaves remarkably like herself—so much that at first I thought it must not be a dream. She started by writing, "I was invited to a picnic (by whom?) (Somewhere in Wheeling)."

She mentioned "food tables" and "people milling around." An awkward conversation with her ex-boyfriend Bruce ensued. She described him as not looking well, and wrote that she cried in front of him—"don't know *why*."

Bruce's presence means this must have been written in the mid-Nineties, I estimate; there is no date marked on the pages. She went on, "At some point the subject of drinking came up. I danced around the topic when people joked about how I loved beer. I was becoming very uncomfortable." Someone in the dream offered her wine, and wouldn't leave her alone, so, "Finally, I took him aside and tried to tell him swiftly to stop it. He kept asking me + teasing me to have some wine. A small crowd was gathering. Finally I said loudly 'no, I don't drink anymore. I've had enough alcohol to float a ship in my lifetime, so I thought I'd give someone else a shot.' People laughed—and I felt relieved."

The manager persisted, saying, "'You're not an alcoholic. Of course you can drink!'"

Posy: "'Okay, I choose not to because it will kill me.'"

This dream-Posy was, of course, correct.

Later in the dream, one man forced another man's head through a wooden box with sharp metal rods arrayed throughout it, so that his head was sliced apart, very slowly, while he screamed and Posy couldn't help him.

~

One of Robert Lowell's poems, "Father's Bedroom," depicts—what else—the contents of his father's bedroom, with particular attention to "volume two / of Lafcadio Hearn's / *Glimpses of an unfamiliar Japan.*" "Its warped olive cover," he writes, "was punished like a rhinoceros hide. / In the flyleaf: / 'Robbie from Mother.'" Another note, left later, tells that the book "'was left under an open / porthole in a storm.'"

    There the poem ends. The first time I read it, as soon as I reached the last line, I wrote a note in the margin, asking myself in pencil, "what is it?" After Posy died, I understood "it" perfectly; an inscription in a book owned by a dead relative is exactly the sort of thing that fascinates an inheritor. It declares that the object has a history, at the same time that it merely suggests that history. With the space it takes up, the inherited object brings with it a story that is seldom known in full.

    Lowell's father is conspicuously absent from the description of his room, which makes his death unmistakably present. The first time I read it, I missed the significance of this. But it is the thing that makes the poem significant.

~

In Posy's living room sat her garden journal, in which, in her final years, she'd kept a faithful record of all that went on in the ground outside her windows.

    As much time as I spent in them growing up, laboring on my mother's behalf, gardens have never really interested me, but the journal of this one did. When I came across it, I turned to the last entry, made two weeks before its author died. "I'll have to put deer-off on all of my plants, to preserve them for the winter," she wrote. "Better to be safe now than sorry later."

    This, like many of the things in Posy's house, took on a rather great significance as soon as she wasn't living.

    Her final garden journal entry was not a passing concern scrawled in a notebook. It was evidence that Posy intended to be at home for at least one more growing season, that she had plans to live longer than she did.

Significance was also granted, suddenly, to a wooden chair that Posy had bought in Pennsylvania. Made of thin slivers of wood, it folded up like the fingers of two hands. Fragile and useless for sitting, it took up too much space, but I associated it so much with Posy, who demonstrated its folding action for me every time I came to see her, that I agreed to take it when no one else would. Eventually I changed my mind, and it went to auction with most of her stuff, but for a while, because Posy had owned it, it was indispensable.

This was also true of the strange ceramic dish in her cupboard, which she had probably made in the Seventies, and which was actually two dishes that came together to contain something—what it was meant to hold we could not determine. It wasn't pretty, but we could tell that Posy had made it, so it broke my heart when no one kept it. I felt the same way for the wooden lap desk she had bought two years before; for the jug she had bought from a Wheeling artist that had a grotesque alligator head for a mouth at its top; and for the book of stories by Woody Allen that sat at her bedside when she died, which I'd inscribed from me to her the prior Christmas, then forgotten.

No one in the family felt we had to keep or take care of Angel, a cat Posy had practically had on life support for twelve years.

Out of all the people in the world, Posy was the only one had liked Angel. The cat barely moved, most of the time—a big, gray lump of fur, and an angry one. Angel would go out of her way to attack any stranger who came near her. I learned in my first visit to Posy's that I had to give the cat a wide berth. She often slashed Posy's skin, and bit her, but the faithful owner held on.

In the days between Posy's death and her body's discovery, Angel spilled cat food throughout the bedroom and pissed on the floor. When Posy was found dead, Angel was found perched dutifully beside her. After Posy died, Angel stayed at the veterinarian's for a few days, but we were advised to have her put to sleep. She was old and sick, and it was what we wanted to hear, anyway.

Only my eldest brother Sam hesitated. He suggested we should maybe keep her alive, at which point we shook our heads and David talked him out of it.

~

"I shall never get you put together entirely," says the speaker of "The Colossus," by Sylvia Plath, to her father. He is now a giant, broken statue, one she has dutifully "Pieced, glued, and properly jointed." He has become a thing that she must maintain. "Scaling little ladders with gluepots and pails of Lysol," Plath writes that she crawls "like an ant in mourning / Over the weedy acres of your brow / To mend the immense skull-plates and clear / The bald, white tumuli of your eyes." It seems that she is bound to carry on in these tasks forever. She shall never get him put together, but she will try.

The Colossus is the speaker's father and her inheritance. He is a monolith she cannot abandon, to which she is bound. "Nights," she tells him, "I squat in the cornucopia / Of your left ear."

This is the most heartbroken of all depictions of the plight of the inheritor. The speaker in this poem is not squatting by the Colossus's lips to see what he might say; she is in his ear, as if he might hear her when she murmurs to him.

But there is no chance of that. He is dead; he is in ruins. It is the wish of the survivor that she might be heard by the departed, when she addresses him. Not even in poetry can that really take place.

~

Amid all of this, I heard from Valerie, an ex-girlfriend I had not seen in years. Just as I no longer lived in Wheeling, she did not still reside in her hometown, an hour's drive away. She lived on a boat, with a man, off the east coast of America. She was home for a little while, though, because the house of some friends of hers had burnt down, taking all of their possessions with it. They had to start over, and Valerie explained to me in an e-mail that she was soliciting help on their behalf, from all her friends and ex-friends, in the form of money and useful things.

In this I saw an opportunity.

Throughout the process of emptying Posy's house, I had maintained a large cardboard box in the basement, filling it with useful things no one wanted. By the time I heard from Valerie, it was brimming with odds and ends: a salad stirrer, a coffee grinder, mixing bowls, a serving dish, and other things I can't remember, but which took up space and might have seemed vital, I realized, to those who had nothing.

And there were other unclaimed things in the house, like a television and some lamps. They would be auctioned for very little money, unless I handed them off to Valerie.

I told her I had these things, and that I would gladly bring them to her if she wanted.

I had an ulterior motive for wanting to see her.

I wasn't secretly still in love with her after all those years; Stefanie and I would marry in six months, and I didn't want to complicate that. Rather, I had recently finished writing something that featured Valerie prominently. I wanted to ask her if I should use her real name or invent an alias, and I preferred to ask her in person.

It was not to be. The day before I was supposed to go see her, and bring her the assorted household items, she wrote and said she'd come down with the flu, and had been violently throwing up, prior to writing. I wouldn't get to see her, which I imagined was for the best, considering my general preference to not make Stefanie jealous. Valerie asked if she could come get Posy's discarded things at a later date, but no, I told her, there wasn't time. We had to clear out Posy's house, and soon. So instead of taking these things to the most desperate people I had recently heard of, we took the kitchen implements and other things to Goodwill, which, I reasoned, was only slightly less benevolent than giving them to a couple of strangers whose house had just burnt down.

~

Stuck with tape to a page in one of Posy's yellowed journals was a generous lock of four inches of her hair. The journal was from 1976, when she was living in England with her husband as he attended Cambridge. The hair, therefore, had made at least one transatlantic voyage in its existence, certainly once when it crossed the ocean in the journal, perhaps once before then when it was growing out of Posy's head.

The hair is a relic of my aunt, but of my aunt as I never knew her. When the scissors—and who knows what happened to those—severed these hairs from her head, my birth was still five years in the future. The hair, though, is unmistakably Posy's. I recognized it like I would her face, if she walked into the room as I write this. How I wish she could.

134

I would say the hair smells like her, but all the journals and their contents smell like her.

I wondered, when I found the hair, if Posy imagined that someone would ever uncover it there. She would not have imagined me finding it, when she taped it down; we hadn't met yet. She probably didn't picture its discovery at all; if she had, she might have wondered what I—or someone else—would do with it, when I found it. I have a feeling Posy didn't think that far ahead, even as she paradoxically set her hair aside for posterity, with a description of the haircut that produced it.

When I found Posy's hair, it occurred to me that it must be the most substantial accumulation of her previously living body left in the world. Perhaps a fingernail or eyelash persisted in the corner of her bedroom, despite the thoroughness with which we cleaned it, but the rest of her burned soon after she died.

Thanks to the hair she taped into her journal in 1976, Posy was there in the room with me in 2009. It wasn't anything like when she was alive; she wasn't whole. But a part of her was, quite literally, present.

It is there still, in my basement, in a crate.

~

"There's been a Death, in the Opposite House," begins one of Emily Dickinson's poems, and in it

> The Neighbors rustle in and out—
> The Doctor—drives away—
> A Window opens like a Pod—
> Abrupt—mechanically—
>
> Somebody flings a Mattrass out—
> The Children hurry by—
> They wonder if it died—on that—
> I used to—when a Boy—

Dickinson describes a post-death cleanup effort that could just as easily be an account of what happened at Posy's house. She mentions "the Man / Of the Appalling Trade" who comes "To take the measure of the House." I think he is the auctioneer, come to decide the value of ordinary things and ensure that they find their way into other hands.

I was there at Posy's on the day our auctioneer came to carry the last of her things away. He and a couple of teenagers—maybe his sons—pulled their truck into the semicircle driveway and began piling things in. Dozens of boxes sat stacked in the living room. I didn't know what they had in them; I didn't want to know. I was taking away from there more things than I needed, as it was. I didn't want to spot more desirable stuff and add it to my cargo.

What interested me far more than what the auctioneer took was what he didn't take. In one of Posy's spare bedrooms the discards were piled: lamps, a television, a portable DVD player, a wooden display case—all deemed valueless by someone practiced in the art of easing burdens placed on inheritors.

I didn't have a chance to talk to the auctioneer—I was busy helping the adolescents carry off my aunt's relics—but I might have asked him how many auctions he had put on that month, or what other estates looked like, piled up in other rooms in other parts of town.

~

Groaning beneath the weight of Posy's estate, my siblings and I divided and carried off our shares.

David hired a truck, loaded into it everything that was to be his, my sister's, and my younger brother's, and hauled it off to the town where they lived in different houses. I was absent for that event, but I heard that David, an organized man, dragged everything to the driveway on a cold, sunny January morning, maneuvering the huge buffet, the library table, and everything else that would fit, into the back of the truck, leaving our aunt's estate more dismantled. My brother Sam hired a team of movers to do this with his new stuff. I don't think Jim took enough to require a truck.

By the time I arrived at the end of January, to hire a U-Haul and cart off my share of new possessions, Posy's house was a shell. "It doesn't feel like Posy's anymore," I told my mother. "It feels like just an empty house."

She agreed, and was as glad to see this as I was. I said it felt better to be in the empty house than it did to be in a house stuffed with Posy's stuff. Again my mother agreed.

Still the house was not completely empty, nor were we close to being through with it. The house would have to be sold, and before that could happen it had to be readied for sale.

I was preparing to drive home to Missouri, in a rented truck laden with my inheritance, but I knew I would have to return many times, to help make Posy's house something someone else would want to take off our hands.

I went to the house with my mother for one last morning of work before I left. We plunged into Posy's basement and found previously unknown, heavy boxes full of stuff Posy had had no reason to bring to Wheeling from D.C., as she must not have used any of it since the mid-Nineties, like a broken record player and lawn fixtures I had never seen on her lawns.

We cleaned out Posy's upstairs linen closet. We disposed of hand towels and bath towels, plus things that don't necessarily belong in a linen closet. We sorted them into bags, and in their midst I found a deeply yellowed, crumpled, torn piece of notebook paper. On it was a poem. It read,

> What song are you singing now, and
> Who are you singing it to?
> How many more souls will be burdened
> With the pain of loving you?
>
> In the sunlight I find myself saying
> Over and over again
> The right man, but the wrong time
> The wrong woman at the right time.

When I exhumed this forgotten manuscript, my heart leapt. I thought I'd found something in the house the likes of which I hadn't seen before, something that would make my aunt's last years appear less wasted.

It didn't matter that Posy was not a great, undiscovered poet. I didn't want to be her literary executor; it was enough to have been her nephew.

I wanted, now that she was dead, to find that Posy had had a richer life in Wheeling than all the evidence suggested. I wanted to learn that although we had thought she was carousing in her home she had, all along, been up to something else. If she had spent some time writing poems—even bad poems—it would mean that perhaps she had had a will to live—to live, that is, in the greatest sense of the word; to be a creative, productive, active human being.

All I had found from her last year was an Alcoholics Anonymous journal, in which she kept a record of conversations with her counselor, and other people's thoughts on her addiction.

I had thought, for a moment, that the yellowed poem was a sign of something greater than that. But the paper it was written on looked ancient. She must have written it years before she died. It found its way, somehow, into this bundle of towels, in a house in a town she spent most of the years of her life wanting to be far away from.

~

Posy once told me, in her house in Wheeling, "I love my garden. I hate Wheeling, but I love my house and my garden." She confided that she felt as if, living in her hometown, in a big house by herself, she was waiting there to die.

Before she died, I used to say that if for some reason I moved back to Wheeling I would sink into despair and die a slow, inebriated death. I haven't said it since Posy died, in large part out of respect for her, since she lived out exactly the hypothetical future I was talking about.

I would not want to trivialize her suffering. Also, there is no need now for me to say such a thing. When I said it before Posy's death—and I said it whenever the subject of Wheeling came up—it was like an incantation, a way to ward off one possible future. I thought if I acknowledged this potential fate, perhaps it would not come true.

Now that Posy has lived out one of my greatest fears, now that I know what dejection and resignation look like, I don't feel I need to recite a litany to help me sidestep a certain prolonged variety of death. Or, anyway, I know it couldn't possibly protect me from it.

My feelings toward Wheeling haven't changed, since Posy died. As much as I admire some of the city's architecture, and as much as I miss, at every moment I spend elsewhere, the majestic hills I was raised among, the city stubbornly persists in being the postindustrial wreck that it was for all the years I spent growing up there. Apart from some rare moments of ill-advised nostalgia, I stubbornly persist in wanting to be in or near it as little as possible.

It the poem "In Response to a Rumor That the Oldest Whore-house in Wheeling, West Virginia, Has Been Condemned," James Wright captures Wheeling pretty well. He writes:

> For the river at Wheeling, West Virginia,
> Has only two shores:
> The one in hell,
> The other in Bridgeport, Ohio.

This is a poem that first appeared in a collection in 1968. Posy was then eighteen, perhaps already eager to get away from the place, to embark on the trajectory that would take her far from Wheeling, only to return her there almost forty years later.

Wright might be overstating the case against Wheeling. It isn't hell—though it must have looked like hell when its industries were in full swing, smoke billowing into the sky. Today it has the appearance one would expect of a small town that was built up by iron and steel mills, only to see the mills shut down abruptly, with nothing to take up the economic slack.

Nearly all of the downtown storefronts are empty. Most of the handsome, old buildings are inhabited only by ghosts.

~

For a year, until it was sold, Posy's house was another of the empty buildings. If it did nothing else, it called me back to my hometown, again and again, as it was in constant need of its inheritors' attention. Rooms had to be painted. Electric and heating bills piled up even in its vacancy. Bats took over the second floor, and men were hired to remove them. For months, the smell of cat urine and cigarettes resisted efforts to eradicate them.

Living five-hundred miles to the west, I was absent for many of these problems and their solutions. But as far away as my body was, I returned to the house often enough in dreams that it was like a second home.

The dream house was not an accurate representation of Posy's actual house. It was bigger, with more windows, though the windows were like Posy's real windows—turn-of-the-century portals with elaborate frames.

The dream-house had the same steep, narrow staircase that Posy was once shoved into, but it was longer and led nowhere.

When I dreamed myself into it, I usually got lost in the house, and found someone there who shouldn't have been.

One night, I looked out Posy's window and saw a young man skulking around the property. Because I was dreaming, I was naked and could fly, so I swooped upon him, flapping my arms like a meaty hawk. When we stood face-to-face, he looked at me guiltily, but confessed that he was only looking for bottles he might take to be recycled in town. Posy never recycled, probably not even in her dreams.

The man showed me an empty wine bottle he had found in her trash. He asked if he could keep it.

I dreamed this, no doubt, because when my mother went looking in Posy's trash, soon after she found her body, she found two empty wine bottles and concluded that Posy had, just prior to her death, tried to curb her heavy drinking by switching from vodka to something milder. She thought this must have brought on a withdrawal seizure, that Posy had tried to save herself, and had unwittingly sealed her fate.

~

On one visit to Wheeling, in the spring that followed Posy's death, Stefanie, my mother and I spent a few days working on the house. I caulked. I removed nails from walls where Posy's drawings no longer hung. Stefanie heard the distinct sound of running water, coming from downstairs.

We found half of the basement flooded with several inches of water that flowed from a leak in a pipe that fed the behemoth of a furnace. Next to it sat unopened boxes of Posy's personal things, soaked now with dirty water.

On another Wheeling visit, in the summer, Stefanie and I went over to dust the floors at Posy's. There had been a violent storm, the night before. It had torn large branches off of half the trees in town. Other trees had broken to pieces. Because Wheeling is 75% trees, there were so many affected trunks and branches that it looked in some places like someone had detonated a hydrogen bomb in the middle of town, one that affected only trees.

When I looked out Posy's window to her backyard, I saw that the cable and telephone wires running from the house to the garage were down. Looking closer, I saw that a large branch from the tree in her yard had snapped, taking the wires with it.

My brother had the tree uprooted, at the estate's expense. My mother said—only half-joking—that she began to worry, whenever she and I went to Posy's, as things seemed to go wrong only when I was there.

~

In a dream, my ex-girlfriend Aurora returned. I had broken up with her three years before then, but by surprise she stepped unwelcome into my home, pregnant and accompanied by another man. Behind her followed every member of her populous family—all six of her sisters, their husbands, and her parents. She said she wanted her furniture back. I didn't have her furniture. She went for the dresser I had taken from Posy's house, the child's dresser in which I hoped to keep my child's clothes, when I had a child to wear them. She and the others tried to take it away. I tried to stop them.

In the next dream, the world was flooded over with water, and I had trouble rowing through it in the canoe that the dream provided me. I drifted into a house, where in one room my parents, brothers and sister were gathered. They waited until I was out of my boat and seated. My father, a lawyer, announced that he had drawn up a list of charges against me. He read them aloud with increasing vehemence, until I could not contain myself. I began screaming at the bunch of them, incoherently, trying and failing to communicate my outrage at what they were doing. My father struck me across the face, but I pried from his hands the list of my offenses. I found that it was, in fact, the list I had made of the things I wanted to take from Posy's house.

In yet another dream, I watched a home movie that had been made of Posy when she was young. She was being dragged through a muddy field by a gang of laughing, young, blonde men. Her eyes were fixed on the camera. She wore the same vacant expression she wears in a photo I keep in my desk, one taken of her when she was not quite thirty. I wanted to help her, but couldn't, as she was on film, removed from me by many years. Then I realized I was wrong. She wasn't looking at the camera but through it. She could see me.

~

In January, I flew to Wheeling and packed my inheritance into a rented truck. With it I traveled west, to the house in Missouri I shared with Stefanie, towing behind me a barrister's bookcase, the dresser, the sword, a folder stuffed with some of Posy's artwork, another folder of some of her photographs, a number of things made of silver, a vase, some glassware and a few more things I must be forgetting, plus lawn furniture. I was not carting a corpse to Missouri, but because of where the truck's contents came from—because a death had made me their owner—the trip felt something like a long, one-vehicle funeral procession.

I barreled through Ohio with Posy's former things, and stopped at an Indiana gas station, where, in the long minutes of the truck's refueling, I went to check on my inheritance.

My mother had insisted that the last thing to go in the truck should be her mother's set of sterling silver flatware. Easily the most valuable set of things I now owned, we had found it stowed in Posy's buffet table, in her dining room, and my mother had convinced me to take it. We polished it together, on the morning of my departure, and assembled it in a wooden case, clamping it tight—so we thought—with a cloth belt.

As soon as I unrolled the truck's back door, the silver knives, forks and spoons, and still other utensils—a dozen each—came pouring out, making a sound like glass breaking in slow motion. Not all of the silver pieces hit the ground, but many did as I raced to reassemble my dead grandmother's flatware set, to get it back in the truck and out of sight. I could think of no better way to provoke theft than to scatter a precious mineral across the asphalt of a busy gas station in an unfamiliar place, even if that place was Indiana.

I don't know what my grandmother would have thought, had she seen the way I spilled so many of her once-cherished dining implements out of a truck. I never met her; she died of a brain tumor in her early fifties, before I was born. But I know, because my mother told me, that the silver was once her mother's, and that my mother used it at dinner on a nightly basis as a girl. It was not until she said this that I realized how my mother quite literally grew up with a silver spoon in her mouth. There was one on the dinner table in front of her, anyway, in case she wanted to use it.

Now the silver spoons that were once in the mouths of my mother and grandparents sat beside their clumsy new owner, in a plastic bag on the passenger seat of a rented truck.

~

Soon after Posy's death, for reasons that had nothing to do with her, I was asked to explain why William Cullen Bryant's "Thanatopsis" was the most widely memorized poem of the nineteenth century in America. As I do in too many circumstances, I mumbled for a few seconds. Then I gave a response unworthy of the question—something about the poem's having been the first by an American author to be recognized at once as great. I cited my own love for it, though I knew I could give a better answer if I had more time to think. I spent the next week searching my head for an explanation more compelling.

I would have had an easier time speculating why another poem from the nineteenth century, Edgar Allan Poe's "The Raven," was memorized often—which it was, by readers like Abraham Lincoln and my great-grandfather. It is catchy, and it has the word "nepenthe" in it, which is hard to forget.

"Thanatopsis" has neither of those things, but it does have the supreme appeal of addressing the subject of death. Bryant tells us nothing less than what will happen to us after we've stopped breathing, and his is an altogether different version of that story from those we get elsewhere, like at church.

He starts by acknowledging that we are all afraid to die. He tells us, though, that when our thoughts turn to death and we let our thoughts get the best of us, we should, in so many words, go outside and listen to nature, which has the power to make us feel better. For, as Bryant assures us, when you die,

> Earth, that nourished thee, shall claim
> Thy growth, to be resolv'd to earth again;
> And, lost each human trace, surrend'ring up
> Thine individual being, shalt thou go
> To mix forever with the elements,
> To be a brother to th' insensible rock
> And to the sluggish clod, which the rude swain
> Turns with his share, and treads upon.

You will become nothing more substantial than mulch. It is a distressing picture, and Bryant adds, "The oak / Shall send his roots abroad, and pierce thy mould." Trees will eat you, and you will be powerless to stop them.

> Then Bryant gives us the bright side.
> "Yet not to thy eternal resting place," he writes,

> Shalt thou retire alone—nor couldst thou wish
> Couch more magnificent. Thou shalt lie down
> With patriarchs of the infant world—with kings
> The powerful of the earth—the wise, the good,
> Fair forms, and hoary seers of ages past,
> All in one mighty sepulchre.

Death is not a void but instead a world packed with the very best of humankind. It is a privilege, then, to die, and to join our predecessors housed in the planet we will share with them.

Leave problems of the soul to Plato and Jonathan Edwards; Bryant wants to tell us about dirt, and our decomposed bodies that will be stepped on and mixed together. Bryant's is the story of how a person becomes peat moss, how a charming, funny, living creature dissipates

144

into shovelfuls of indiscriminate earth.

Although I hadn't memorized it, I thought of "Thanatopsis" years ago, at the funeral my friend Bryce. I stood with a handful of friends and his parents, on an obscure hill, lost among trees and hills on the outskirts of my hometown, and together we buried the twenty-one-year-old. I took a long look at the grass, and the lush greenery, and thought that if Bryce's mold was to be pierced by roots then it should be by the roots of these trees, on a hillside so picturesque it could have been the setting for a Bryant poem.

What has concerned me lately, though, is not how a person becomes dirt, but how someone becomes a coffee table, or a wall sconce, or a hundred shares of Johnson & Johnson. After Posy expired before her television, to be cremated one week later, I watched every trace of her, with her little body and enormous presence, dissipate into an inheritance consisting of objects that range in size and importance from a pile of diaries to a house built in the early twentieth century.

These things are not my aunt, as she is now an urn's worth of ashes underground, but all of them share in her, having once been hers, and from them she is inextricable.

~

Posy was not autopsied. She had requested, several weeks before she died, that her body should not be so dissected in the event of her death. So as I dug through the box of Posy's journals—including the one with a lock of her hair stuck inside it with tape—I did my best not to think of her diaries as her body, myself as its reluctant investigator.

In a way, though, it was an apt analogy. I wanted to know what it was that had killed my aunt, and I was turning to her journals for evidence to help me determine this.

I knew, of course, what had caused her death; drinking had done it, slowly and with a lot of pain, but there was more to it than that, I knew, and I thought if I looked in her photographs, her artwork, her journals, and other things, I would find something to indicate why she had resigned herself to living in a big house and waiting for her life to run out. I could, I thought, determine once and for all what it was that had hurried her into her grave.

I looked to Posy's artwork, since I took from her home many works of art she produced. None of them hung on my walls; they languished instead in a large, brown folder in my closet, where no one could see them.

Posy's drawings nearly always depict knights. Whether they gather around a fire, or fight with armor-plated lizards in the wilderness, knights are present throughout Posy's large collection of drawings. In one especially intricate pencil work, titled "Faith, Honor + Courage," a team of them square off against what appear to be mutated reptiles. They are on a drawbridge. One knight aims a spear at a large turtle with claws and a long neck. Another prepares to swing a mace at a flying lizard who swoops down to meet his blow with its claws.

The knights are dressed as crusaders, and wear beards. On their faces are looks of concern. They look as if they might not make it through the present conflict.

I suggested to Stefanie that perhaps we should get this drawing framed. We could, I said, hang it in a child's bedroom someday. We had talked of having children, and although their reality was long away, I had them on my mind.

Stefanie was unconvinced. She didn't seem to consider the drawing to be appropriate for a child's room. I wondered if this disapproval might result from her never having played Dungeons and Dragons.

Another of Posy's drawings features still more knights—two of them, one with his arm on his comrade's shoulder, with a sword hanging from his other hand. His friend looks over at him approvingly. She drew it while she was at work, evidently; her organization's letterhead is to the left of the off-duty knights.

Posy spent her life, it seems, drawing these beknighted scenes. When the knights aren't leaning, they are, like the gang of crusaders, battling dragons and similar creatures. Particulars vary, but every scene consists of essentially the same thing: desperate people in armor with sharp instruments, fending off strange attackers.

I cannot resist projecting onto this Posy's constant effort to subdue those parts of herself that would bring her to ruin; I cannot help but see in her Alcoholics Anonymous journal another iteration of this same struggle. In both, the harried individual takes on forces indomitable and mysterious. The outlook never looks good.

In the study carrel I rented at my Missouri library, I hung a drawing Posy made in pen, of a woman—probably a princess—on an ivy-covered balcony, looking out at something off the page. Since this is one of Posy's drawings, she is probably looking for a knight, or thinking about one. But where I placed her, when I was with her in my carrel, all that she could see was me.

~

Of all the photos we unearthed after Posy died, one has been featured prominently in my mind, in that I thought of it abruptly when waking up in the morning, and when swimming at the local pool. It was taken somewhere in Europe, when Posy was a teenager, and in it she stands with four other youths—three men, and a woman from home who accompanied her on the trip. One of the men smokes a pipe. Another stands with his arm draped over Posy's shoulder, his hand just above her breast. Both men are blonde; I think it may have been taken in Sweden. All of those pictured are young enough that their attempts to look serious fall short, especially the one with the pipe in his mouth.

One of them was a young man named Peter, who for a year after the photo was taken sent Posy politically charged letters and photographs of himself with sideburns of increasing size. He asked Posy if she knew anyone in the Black Panther Party, and declared to her that he would vote them into office, were he an American. He asked her about Angela Davis and said he'd just read Eldridge Cleaver's *Soul on Ice*—which, incidentally, I had read just prior to finding Peter's letter. Eventually, he mailed Posy a Möbius strip with messages on it written in red marker, to the effect that he had decided to join the Communist party.

Another man Posy met in Europe—an Italian named Franco—wrote in one of his many letters to her, "*I hate the communism.*" For several years he sent her Christmas cards and postcards from multiple cities in Europe. He implored her always to return to him, telling her in every other letter how much their brief time together had meant.

I have wondered if these men are still alive. I have thought of what it might be like to track them down. For some reason, of all the men from Posy's life, some of whom I could go and see with relative ease if I wanted to, these Europeans intrigue me most—perhaps because their contact with Posy was fleeting, and because I'd like to know if my aunt made a lasting enough impression that they would remember her still today.

Posy met them in 1967. She was seventeen, and some of the nuns at the Catholic school she attended—despite our family's Protestantism—had arranged the trip to Europe that would remove her from her family for a month and bring her into contact with these men. During that time her father, mother, sister and brother wrote her letters that survived all the years of her life that followed. Posy preserved them in a fat envelope, and kept them in the bosom of a cardboard box.

One letter from her father began, "By the time you get this, your *Romeing* days will be over. I hope you haven't eaten too much so you still have a good forum." He gave consistent updates as to how much Gretel, the family Dachshund, missed Posy, and reported where the dog was in the house as he wrote—for example, "Gretel is sacked out in the music room with half an eye on the door and half an eye on me, to see that I don't get away."

The letters are thoroughly paternal. He wrote, "We have decided that there will be a new name for you, and will select it from the following:—'Old Salt', 'Gob', 'Bell Bottom Trousers', or maybe simply 'Sailor'—for you seem to have a sweetheart in every Port." "Sailor with a Sweetheart in Every Port" became the salutation for all of his letters to follow.

My grandfather also gave consistent updates as to the goings-on among family members at home. "Just as I finished the last sentence," he wrote in a letter, interrupting himself, "Auntie walked in and said that Uncle Ed had raised his head too suddenly in the cellar and bumped into a furnace pipe, so I just got back from the office where we had to put in a stitch. I told Uncle Ed I was running out of things to write about, so now there was some news."

Posy's brother wrote her just one letter, in which he addressed her as a brother does his younger sister, with affection filtered through a rough history of their having had to grow up together. He said he envied her for traveling abroad, but spent most of the letter discussing the hour he'd just spent at the swimming pool. He mentioned that the sun was

148

too hot, and so he had gone inside.

When I came across a letter from my mother I recognized her handwriting at once. But the script is the only thing I recognize. It begins, "June still—but not for long. Because the agonizingly hot days of that pearl of all summer months July—follows swiftly upon the bittersweet languidly hushed and swealtering daze of June which means that another month is shot to—and also that 1/3 of that good ol' summertime is Gone—Baby—Gone." I can hardly believe this is the same woman I have called mother for thirty-plus years, the woman who speaks with great passion about Thomas Jefferson. I realize that anything written by my mother fourteen years before I came into being is bound to seem as if it came from an imposter with my mother's handwriting. Still, I never guessed my mother could write such sentences.

She asks Posy, "How's your dissentary, scurvy and all that coming—(or should say—going! Heh Heh)" She tells her she has recently interviewed at Chatham, a school she would attend briefly. The most important part follows, I suppose: "Christmas is fine—So'm I. still hot and pashionate—us 2. Plans are for me to have a ring sometime around Xmas and 'to be wed' in late summer or early fall of '68—Great—RIGHT?" I assume she is referring to my father; the date matches up with the date of their marriage. She ends the letter, "Well—Have fun and LEARN BABY—LEARN!"

She seems, in this letter, more like Janis Joplin than my mother.

Among other things, these letters indicate what the city of Wheeling once was for people in my family. The city was, at the time, thick with relatives I would like to know but can't because most of them are dead. In her letters, Posy's mother makes repeated references to visits from cousins and other such people. "Grandmother came up this morning to pick up the strawberries," she wrote. "I read your letter to her and she loved it all—Aunt Lil + Aunt Anne took her on a world tour when she was a young woman." The impression I gather from this, and from other such asides, is that life in Wheeling, for my relatives at the time, took place in the cozy context of a large and close family, centered around the hill they occupied together.

Their hill was Chicken Neck Hill, and at the top of it was and still is "The Circle"—a long driveway of sorts that rounds a large, grassy space with a few trees and usually at least one deer. On one side of the hilltop is a steep, wooded incline, and on the other are a set of large houses, all of them owned by members of my extended family. It has been that way for generations, though a couple of the houses had to be taken down twenty years ago, as they were falling apart and no one lived in them anymore.

For much of my young life—after the oblivion of early childhood, anyway—I didn't like going to this place. Now that I'm older, and am not made to stand around feeling awkward there every Easter, I can't help thinking of it as an idyllic haven for those who share my blood.

I can see, through the window that these letters provide, what has always made my hometown appeal to my mother. She was around for our family's heyday, when there were people living next door, and in the next house over, and the next one, who had known her since birth and cared about her.

It is almost enough to make me want to invest in a Missouri hillside, get some unlikely job that would pay good money in a broken economy, and fashion myself into a true patriarch. But it isn't quite enough to make me want to do that, and I doubt that Stefanie would join me. I don't have the right profile to be a patriarch, nor do I have enough money.

~

When Posy was preparing to leave for her trip abroad, someone named Karen wrote her, "Well I did my part getting you home last Friday, so I hope you managed to get upstairs to your room without anyone stepping on your hands. Have a good time in Europe and save some of it for me."

I later learned, from clues left in other letters, that Karen was a teacher at Posy's high school. I found her obituary online; she later became a podiatrist and died in 2008. But in April 1968, she wrote,

> I'm so sorry about your mother, Posy. If there is a malignancy and it is inoperable then you must brace yourself. At the risk of upsetting you I must tell you that it will be absolute hell. I went through it with my father, and even though I hardly knew the man until a few weeks

before he died, it was just awful.

My grandmother was ill and getting worse. She was about to be diagnosed with brain cancer. She would not live long.

One of the letters Posy's mother sent her in Europe looks as if it was written while she sat at a vibrating table, as it appears in a large, almost illegible scribble. In another, typewritten letter she mentioned how much trouble she was having with my grandfather's typewriter. It was not because she wasn't used to it; it was all due to her failing motor skills. She wrote, ominously, "the numbness in my area is back."

In the house where Posy died, I found a yellowed sheet of looseleaf paper. On it Posy mentioned that she couldn't sleep, that she felt as if she couldn't move, that it was as if her insides had been removed. My mother took it, read it, and said that, based on the date inscribed, it was written just after Posy returned from Europe—on the night their mother died.

Other letters from Karen provide an outline of what Posy did after her mother's death. That December, Karen wrote her, "I think you did exactly the right thing by dropping out of school." Posy had found that with the loss of her mother she could not go on at Bethany College, just outside of Wheeling.

"There were things that your mother could have taught you," Karen wrote. "Jokes that could have been shared, sunny days on which she might have enjoyed the fragrance of a flower or watched the squirrels at the window, and many other things. No matter how long a person lives, death always cuts life short."

I don't know what Posy's response to this was, but in her letters Karen's is a constant voice of understanding and reason. It makes me sorry that she is dead; I find it satisfying to think that some of the people who wrote these letters to Posy are still alive and active in the world. Plenty of them are; Posy kept letters from Candace and Marcia—people I don't recall ever meeting, but who were present in her life until the end.

Their letters have sat in a pile in a box beside my desk, doing what they did for all the years that Posy had them, at least at those times when I am not reading and copying parts of them.

I know that I could return the letters to their authors, rather than keep them in my closet at home. I could hand them over and tell them they could do with them what they liked.

I have been tempted to do this every time I've looked at them since I brought them to my house. At the same time, it would seem to make more sense to do what once was customary: burn the lot of them. They were meant for Posy, and when she died they were made redundant.

But I haven't torched them or thrown them away. I have kept them, and read them, despite what their authors or Posy might think of that.

~

Posy died knowing I was engaged to Stefanie, but she didn't live long enough to get a wedding invitation. Her absence from the world, then, did not cause a gap to inhabit a front pew at the tiny chapel in Kansas City where forty people watched us take our vows.

Instead, on my wedding day, my mother handed me a little frog made of marble, the size of one joint of my thumb. When I was twenty-one I brought it home to Posy as a souvenir from a trip to Ireland. Posy had attached to it a little note, stating as much. Without that, I wouldn't have connected it with myself. I had forgotten it altogether.

I carried the frog in a pocket of the grey suit I wore on my wedding day. It was there to greet my hand when I fished for Stefanie's ring, with everyone watching. To the extent she could, then, although she was long gone, Posy had a presence there. A trace of her remained.

Two days later, I flew with Stefanie to Barcelona, for a honeymoon, which I knew I could afford because Posy had named me in her will and she was dead.

The pitchers of sangria we drank, the dinners we ate—earlier in the evening, it seemed, than anyone else in Spain ate dinner—and the night we sat up in our hotel room watching a bad American film we never would have sat through in America, were all posthumous gifts from Posy.

Soon after the honeymoon, I began having dreams about money. Lots of people have these, I understand, and I have had many of my own, in which I win the lottery and get happy, or find a great sum of currency and keep it. Typically I wake from these dreams disappointed, bereft of the fortune that had been mine seconds before.

My new dreams were different. In one, I went to an ATM and made a withdrawal from my bank account, but withdrew too much by mistake. Hundreds of dollars in mixed bills poured from the machine slipped out of my hands. I fled, failing to hold the money together, afraid to draw attention to myself. I chided myself aloud for having probably overdrawn my bank account.

I didn't want the money, in the dream. It was a problem, and taking it had been a mistake.

~

Posy was a wealthy woman. I had known this prior to her death, but hadn't thought about it much, and never went as far as to wonder just how much money she had stashed away. During the cleanup at her house, I learned, from glancing at bank documents with a paper shredder beside me, that from her aunt Catherine, and from her father, she had inherited a modest fortune. She was not quite but almost a millionaire.

She had had a relatively great sum of money and had not been happy.

I know that money can't buy happiness; it can't even buy love. But it doesn't exactly impede happiness, and although it gives me the occasional nightmare, in waking life I find it can resolve certain problems—bills among them—as nothing else can.

Within weeks of receiving the first installment of my inheritance, I paid off my student loans. They were not staggering, but they amounted to more than ten thousand dollars. I resolved them merely by writing a check, and I didn't have to work longer hours in order to do it, or donate plasma, or spend less money at bars. Money cannot buy happiness, but my limited experience indicates that it can bribe happiness to come a little nearer than it might otherwise be inclined to.

I have always thought that someone who has a great deal of money should do a particular set of things with it. One is donate to secular charities. Another is travel the world. I don't know Posy's charity record, but I know she didn't travel, at least not the way a moderately wealthy person with no children has the freedom to do.

She could have gone to France. She could have spent ten years in France. Instead, when she went to the trouble of relocating from D.C., she moved to Wheeling, stayed put, and drank. She hadn't had to do any of those things.

~

On one of my trips home, in the year after Posy died, I retrieved her diaries from the basement in Pittsburgh where my brother Jim had stored them. They were in several large boxes beside the debris his ex-wife left when they divorced some years before. I put them in the trunk of my car and drove them to Missouri.

Posy kept many journals throughout her life. She appears to have saved them all, along with every other written document she produced. If she made a note on looseleaf paper, she stuck it between the pages of her current journal. If she wrote someone a letter, she photocopied it for her records. She saved notes, letters and post cards that were mailed to her by lovers, my mother, their father, and a handful of people I never met. She documented everything. The reason for this is not altogether clear.

But, as Joan Didion has explained, in her essay "On Keeping a Notebook," "The impulse to write things down is a peculiarly compulsive one, inexplicable to those who do not share it, useful only accidentally, only secondarily, in the way that any compulsion tries to justify itself."

Notebooks, she says, are made of "bits of the mind's string too short to use, an indiscriminate and erratic assemblage with meaning only for its maker."

If Didion was right, and she usually is, then the journals were meant for their author's use, and hers alone. They could serve their real purpose no longer, without Posy there to reread or continue writing in them.

If I read Posy's journals, I thought, it might mean crossing a line that should not be crossed. It might—it would—mean violating a dead woman's privacy.

I thought the right thing to do might be to put the journals in a large pile, someplace far from a dry, forested area, douse them with

154

lighter fluid, and set them ablaze—perhaps, for form's sake, with a lighter from Posy's kitchen.

Instead I read every diary, cover to cover.

I was curious, on the one hand, to know Posy, now that she was dead; I had known her well in life, but only as a nephew knows his aunt. I expected the diaries to cover a number of things, such as her eleven-year marriage, her subsequent relationships, and the 1980s, that she never discussed with me in depth. If I learned more about these things, I thought, then I might come to understand my aunt better in death than I did when she lived.

So I dove right in. I picked a notebook at random, in my library carrel, and began invading the privacy of the deceased.

An hour after I started to read the diaries, I still didn't know what had killed her, but I felt as if I had been punched in the stomach by a strange hydraulic machine, and would not recover from the blow for a long time.

I blamed this on the content of one journal from 1970. It started as a notebook for one of Posy's art classes at Wheeling College, and swiftly became a record of the problems she was having with David, who was not yet her husband but would be soon.

The entries are addressed to him, though I doubt he ever read them; I think it was merely a stylistic choice, like when poets write poems addressed to their parents who are already dead. She argues with him, on paper that he was never to read, that he is unfair to her, and that he wrongs her often, in subtle and unsubtle ways. She knows what it means when he disappears on his birthday with a friend of theirs—a woman—and doesn't return until late the next day. She stayed up all night, watching for him out of her window.

The natural response to reading this—her effort to sort out her problems on paper—was to wish that I could help. But there was no helping Posy; her problems were between two and four decades old by the time I found them, and she was gone.

There is something terribly masochistic in reading a dead woman's diary, and I soon understood why it once was customary—perhaps it is still—to burn private letters, journals, and papers, as soon as their author expired. It is when you read a dead person's private writing that that person seems the most dead.

~

Many of the diaries are predictably dull. Posy made the same mistake I made for the seven years I spent keeping journals: devoted all of her attention to things that appeared enormously important at the time of writing, but which were, in retrospect, or in the eyes of another reader, trivial. Posy wrote mostly about relationships with men, and her moods, which were usually low. It is rare for this to be worth the attention of an audience. Exceptions are striking.

One of the diaries begins in June of 1985, six months into its author's relationship with Lawrence, the wealthy man with stark white hair. The notebook must have been a gift from him, as it begins with his instructions:

> Posy dear,
>   Write about us,
>   we *will* make
>   history.
>   You are a wonderful
>   person! My love!
>   Lawrence

The journal documents the end of their relationship, as he grows distant and my aunt appears to fall apart. She and Lawrence made love on some evenings; on others they fought. She fell in love with his house.

She preserved a fortune cookie that read, "You have a long-term stimulation relative to business."

She told him she loved him.

He met her parents. He then spent a weekend without her with his young children, at his farm in Maryland.

He spent another weekend there with a lover from his distant—but not too distant—past. As he let things cool off in this way, Posy saw a doctor for a valium prescription and lost sixteen pounds in two weeks.

Lawrence gave her a series of checks with her therapist's name on them, and eventually gave her a blank check with her name on it. She didn't know how to interpret that. A friend suggested she "take

156

him to the cleaners." I cannot help noting that if she had, it might have increased my recent inheritance.

Posy spent a night drinking alone, and as her valium wore off she fell, breaking a toe and splitting her lip. She spent a lot of time pleading with Lawrence on the pages of a diary she knew he would never read, telling him she wanted their lives to work together. They wouldn't.

By September, Posy knew where things with Lawrence were going, noting his failure to tell her that he loved her—except one time, when he was "under pressure" to do it. On the day that marked nine months of their affair, he went to see a distant cousin he had always been in love with, to see if he still loved her. He claimed it was an experiment, but of course it was the start of his next love affair. Meanwhile, my mother miscarried, delaying by a few more years the birth of her sixth child.

Posy came to Wheeling, to visit. There she wrote, still addressing Lawrence, though writing to herself, "Rob asked if he could go to your farm again. And would I be there..."

I was four. Posy and my parents had taken me to Lawrence's farm some months before, for the first of two visits I would make to his rural home. I have only the faintest memories of the first trip, but Posy kept a handful of photographs from it. In one, I am being upbraided by Lawrence. Only the back of my head is visible as I stand attentive, small and upright, on a patio at night. Lawrence, with his white hair and executive face, furrows his eyebrows at me, disappointed.

I remember why he looked at me this way. He had taken me with him to run an errand, and had stopped somewhere to buy taffy— which I was to share, he decreed, with my elder brother Jim. I didn't want to share it, partly because I was a selfish child, but also because I simply felt that Jim should not have any of my taffy. To this day, I maintain that position.

I threw some degree of a tantrum. Lawrence scolded me. I recall distinctly the shock of being so treated by a stranger, and the gratitude with which my parents yielded to him.

I don't know if I knew Posy was taking my picture, and I wonder now why she did. Perhaps she was impressed with Lawrence's fatherly initiative. I know, from my mother and from Posy's diaries, that she adored him.

The second time I went to Lawrence's farm was in 2004. I had traveled to D.C. to make one of my visits to Posy. We took a day trip to see Lawrence at his rustic home, where I hadn't been in nineteen years. I didn't recognize the farm, but I recognized Lawrence, with his unmistakable, stark, white hair, and only then did it dawn on me that I had once been to this place. We toured his historic, multimillion-dollar farmhouse. I drove around on a cart with some children I had never met, whose relationship to Lawrence I don't recall the nature of—they must have been grandchildren.

When I returned with the children, to find Lawrence and Posy standing close together, looking into each other's eyes, Lawrence offered me a beer, but upon inspection it turned out that the keg in his fridge had gone dry. He offered to let me ride his old motorcycle—something I'd never tried to do—but the vehicle wouldn't start. It was probably for the best, Posy admitted, as someone might have held her accountable, had my head caved in on the side of the road due to a motorcycle accident on a farm near a pond where I had, at the age of four, caught five fish in one outing. Nineteen years later, I tried fishing again in the same pond, with the children, but the line snapped as soon as I had one hooked. The kids were upset with me, as there were no other hooks on the farm.

For a while after their affair, Posy and Lawrence would continue to meet from time to time at the National Cathedral, for talking and "necking." One night when it was warm enough, he brought his mini-TV and they watched Cheers together in the Rose Garden.

Between pages of her diary, Posy inserted some photos she and Lawrence took of each other in the winter they spent together. In one, she stands in a scarf, sweater and jacket before a snow-covered lawn, and looks into the camera with what appears to be amused incredulity. Her brow furrows, and her lips curl, as if she is about to tell Lawrence to put away his camera.

I returned to the photo often when reading Posy's diaries. I liked to think she might react with the same face as this, if she could see me digging through her personal writing like I was; that she would be amused in death by my fascination with her life.

When I mentioned to friends that I was spending my days poring over my dead aunt's journals, they made faces more like the face I suspect Posy would have made if she could have seen me reading her life's work. Their expressions betrayed either mild disgust or disinterested puzzlement—I could not decide which, and didn't ask which. Mostly, I tried to avoid mentioning my work to other people.

~

At the end of the Lawrence affair, Posy went to see her friend Marcia in San Francisco. She wrote that Marcia

> says people mistakenly believe that San Fran has lots of joggers. Actually they're inappropriately dressed tourists who find they can't stop on the 'downhill' walk on some of these miniature mountains. Hence, you see young and old alike, clad in shorts, careening like bullets down the streets (the cameras, of course, are a dead giveaway). I, on the other hand, simply sit down and slide. (Saves on my shoes but it's hell on my trousers)

Learning that Posy made this trip explained her reaction to the trip I made there in my early twenties. Desperately trying to recover from a breakup I initiated clumsily and immediately regretted, I sought in California the phantom cure of geography. After two weeks spent wandering the city—which is exactly what Posy did eighteen years before, and for similar reasons—I flew to D.C., and spent a few weeks with Posy. I learned from her that while I was gone, she and my mother had speculated by phone that I would meet one of two fates: either I would be recruited on the street by someone from a modeling agency, thanks to my good looks, which I have never believed in, or for the same reason I would be drugged by a gang of slick, underhanded homosexuals, and they would rape me.

I understand now why Posy thought the latter event might happen. Although she found San Francisco charming, praising her Scotch-Irish legs for being made for the hills, throughout her week in the city she found its people alarming, even frightening. In her journal she wrote that the city was full of "crazies" who "appear to outnumber the sane people—all the time, everywhere."

At one point, Posy considered moving to San Francisco for good, as it might have improved Marcia's mental condition—she offers no details on that. She admitted that the place was fascinating, and that D.C. was boring in comparison.

I can't help it: I wonder how much longer she might have lived, had she lived there.

~

From Posy's diaries I was coming to a new understanding of Posy, and of the man she loved who scolded me when I was four.

Her 1986 journal makes passing references to the devastation Lawrence ultimately left her in, and the drinking she did in the ruins of their affair. She resolved, over and over, to be alone and heal herself, but she wrote on Valentine's Day, about Lawrence, "Mentally I killed him many times. Obliterating his life from this earth forever." Then she wondered on paper if she could ever marshal the wherewithal to murder him. She considered enlisting her friend Gloria in the cause.

It is a side of Posy I never saw—which seems right enough, as we were blood relatives and not criminal accomplices.

In an entry from December 1985, Posy wrote that she had recently asked a favor of Lawrence—one he promised he would never fulfill. She wanted to be "cremated, but not buried," and scattered over Lawrence's farm, by Lawrence and whomever he was with at the time—I assume she meant whatever woman he was dating.

Of course that didn't happen. She admits, further in the entry, "Perhaps I should want to lie next to my mother at Greenwood."

And there she was put, twenty-four years later.

~

On the Easter that followed her breakup with Lawrence, Posy went to the National Cathedral to pray. There she met Bruce. Immediately she fell for Bruce. She wondered, on the pages of her journal, without a trace of irony, if he was sent to her by God. He wasn't; a divine emissary would not have given her a birthday card, one month after they started sleeping together, which doubled as a breakup note. Posy preserved it

160

in her journal.

Posy swiftly got involved with Bruce, thinking him an answer to her despairing prayers. Then he left her. Then he returned. He repeated the cycle several more times. She wrote, "I feel like Esmerelda in 'The Hunchback of Notre Dame.' I'm a lovely woman in the midst of misfits."

I have long believed in the importance of examining one's life, but Posy's fat envelope marked "Letters to the Brucester" has led me to doubt the practice. It contains unsent letters to Bruce written mostly in 1986. Bruce was, it appears, a man who drove and loved a Porsche; who did modeling work to supplement his income doing something at NASA that Posy didn't specify; who kept Posy at a distance most of the time and expected her to be cheerful when they were together—as she tells it, anyway.

It isn't her own life Posy examined in her letters to him, I suppose. Rather, she examined Bruce's life, recording every false move he made when they were together, such as his refusal to engage her in conversation and how rude he was to her friends.

The most concise document I have found in the envelope is a list Posy made of Bruce's pros and cons. She listed a series of qualities in opposing columns, and ranked Bruce on a scale of one to ten. In the "pros" category, he scored a perfect ten for being "good lookin'" and for his understanding of finances. She gave him nines for intelligence, gentleness, values, and honesty—but he got a four for "caring" and a borderline three and four for "curiosity." His "cons" were rather damning, as he didn't like children, and wasn't "romantic," "spontaneous" or "social." He didn't dress or eat well, scoring a four on both. His "losing his hair" score was four verging on five, written as the fraction 4/5. For "belligerent" and "moody" she gave him a nine—which I assume means he was decidedly both of those things.

To be fair to Bruce, Posy put him in some unpleasant circumstances. When they were dating, she still saw Lawrence often; he took her out for sushi from time to time, since his current lover didn't like sushi. Everyone at the office was invited to Lawrence's farm for his fortieth birthday, and Posy begged Bruce to go with her. He refused to tag along, and I can see why.

My mother urged Posy to go alone, thinking her sister might

meet someone better than Bruce, a pleasant, wealthy friend of Lawrence who might behave more acceptably when others were around.

Everyone, it seems, advised Posy to keep away from Bruce, but she refused to give up on him, despite how she compared herself to a puppy who returns many times to the owner who beats it.

In one of her letters to Bruce, Posy mentions attending a reception for a Haitian singer who had just released a new album. He gave her a signed copy of the record to take home, and she took it home. Then, twenty years later, she moved it with her to Wheeling. Four years after that, I brought it with her other records to Missouri. The singer's signature is prominent on its sleeve; it reads, "To Posy one of the wonders of the world." He is Haitian, and as earnestly as he sings his signature tune it sounds like pretend music to me, like it isn't even real music.

I found a reference, in "Letters to the Brucester," to some dirty pictures Posy picked up at the drugstore one afternoon. They were taken in her living room. She wrote, after retrieving the photos from having them developed, "Harrumph!" At least one of the photos depicted Bruce's erect penis in close-up; I know this because I found these same photos at the house Posy died in.

When I pulled them out of their resident shoebox I had a paper shredder beside me; as soon as I recognized what the photos were of, I did not say "Harrumph!" I sent them through the machine.

The story told in "Letters to the Brucester" consists of the same chain of events, repeated many times, over the course of roughly one year. Posy and Bruce make passionate love, and she gazes at him as he sleeps, longing for a deeper commitment. She admires his legs and arms. She tells him she loves him, and then doesn't see him for several days, or a week, or longer. He returns, and these events, or others like them, recur, until he suggests they move in together.

They don't, but he stays at her house often. As they stand together before her bathroom mirror one night, he asks her to marry him, but when she says yes he insists he was speaking hypothetically, and maintains that he meant only to see how she would respond to the question.

Posy's ultimate conclusion, reached in May of 1987, was that Bruce cared more about things—his Porsche most of all—than he cared about people. When I read this, it occurred to me that I, surrounded at home by Posy's things, poring over her diaries, was also preoccupied with things, with inanimate stuff, but for different reasons; now that Posy was dead, all I had of her were things. I supposed I had memories, too, but those are more fickle than things.

Near the end of writing her "Letters to the Brucester," Posy reread some entries from her old diaries. It was exactly what I had been doing.

In one of the Letters, she transcribed an earlier diary entry that was written on the day she met Bruce at the National Cathedral. In that entry, she described opening the Book of Common Prayer to an auspicious passage she doesn't specify.

Then she transcribed another entry, written one week after the first. It read,

> I woke up at 3:30 am from a dream. I was standing alone in a bare room—white or off white walls. I was aware I was being judged—and I was standing a long time before a voice said "You won't be around much longer. You're going to die soon."
>
> Crying, I begged to live longer. "I have so much to do—people to reach. I have to learn more."
>
> Then I felt as if my request were being considered, although I got no reply.

I had previously found the same journal entry myself, and had transcribed it just as Posy had. Like Posy, I had found it significant, but for altogether different reasons. I was struck by the utterly serious way she presaged her death, which seemed incredibly significant now that she had died.

Posy mentions her death many times throughout her diaries, and whenever she does I find it arresting.

I admit it is a little absurd of me to find my aunt's written anticipations of death more significant after her death than I would have had I read them before it. Posy was not predicting something she had any reason to doubt would eventually take place, so that to consider her death dream prophetic is like considering it profound that this morning I felt certain that in a matter of hours night would come again. It would only be truly remarkable if it turned out never to happen.

Still, I can't help feeling funny when Posy ruminates on her own death, in part because I have been ruminating on it, too. The suddenness of her death seems to make it worthy of premonition. I do not think I would have this reaction if she died ten years from now, of causes more natural.

~

Aside from herself, Posy is concerned in her diaries with no one more consistently than my mother—who is, because of my relationship to her, the person whose presence on these pages fascinates me most. I never would have imagined that in the early Eighties my mother read Toni Morrison's *Tar Baby*, then transcribed an excerpt many pages long and mailed it to Posy. This is because I was two when she did it, but aside from that it seems dramatically unlike my mother—who, for as long as I can remember, has almost exclusively read books about the Founding Fathers.

I suppose this is the fate of many people; we think we know our parents for years, until someday we read diaries written by the dead people who knew them better and gain a dramatically new perspective.

Posy seems to be at her best when writing about my mother, and I suspect this is mostly because it means she is not engrossed in her own problems. When my mother has a miscarriage, when she breaks down on the phone because she is raising her first four children with no help from my father, and when she is left in Wheeling with an ailing father, conniving stepmother, and two siblings who live hundreds of miles away and rarely visit, Posy is forced to devote some space in her journal to someone else's trouble, to a life not her own. Her problems were important, and worth her attention, but when she is explicitly concerned for others I see something in her I don't see elsewhere.

Posy wrote in her diaries regardless of her mood, and there are entries in which she does things other than worry for herself and try to reason out urgent problems with her love affairs. She marvels, in her own way, at flowers, at the perceived work of angels, and at the beauty of the National Cathedral. She is, at times, funny, and at other times perfectly elated. In an entry from June 1983, written just after her divorce,

164

she wrote, "My name has changed. Many documents to update…I feel good about being Posy H_____ again. More than 100%. I've found being alone and making my own decisions a necessary, difficult, but oddly rewarding experience."

I believe her. Although her satisfaction was not to last, it attests to how happy she could be, something she rarely recorded on paper.

~

In August of 1990, Posy began a new diary. She and my mother had just finished reading the 1840s journal of one of our ancestor, and both felt as if they knew the long-dead man personally. "Perhaps," Posy wrote, "if I try to keep some sort of record of my feelings, the events of the time, at some future date, someone may come across this and get to know me." She had apparently forgotten the reams of paper she had already filled with such records, and then wrote, "Is that ego talking? Maybe so. Many people 'stay alive' through their children, and grandchildren. Through my own choosing, I have no children, and can only hope that my nephews and niece will remember me. That is probably a short run proposition."

I should not make too much of this statement, as it is only something Posy scribbled in passing as she and I, from our separate vantages, watched our military prepare to invade the Persian Gulf.

Still, this entry meant that perhaps I was not, when reading her journals, an unwelcome inquisitor, but an invited audience.

She had named me as someone she wanted to remember her. I was doing my job.

"Anne called today," Posy wrote of my mother that September, to relate an unsettling experience. She'd 'inherited' Dad's plastic pill calendar and decided to put [it] on her kitchen window and actually *use* it. All the kids except Will were in school when she decided to pack up + go to the store. When she got back with Will + the groceries she noticed the date had changed back to Sunday, May 20.'

That was, of course, the date of their father's death.

The occurrence itself is less significant to me than what it says about Posy—that inheritance was as troubling for her as it is for me now. Just as Posy seems to persist in her things, her father appeared to her and my mother through what once belonged to him.

My mother woke in the middle of the night soon after their father died, and felt his presence.

Some months later, a flood struck Wheeling, as they do, and every basement on the block filled with water—except hers. Her father's library had been moved there upon his death. My mother saw in this her father's continued influence over his cherished things.

"I'm envious of these occurrences," Posy wrote, "even though she says she's spooked by them."

When, in January 1991, Posy noted that the U.S. had started bombing targets in Iraq, Bruce was still in her life. Four months later, just before her birthday, she wrote, "I'm too depressed to go on. Bruce is the only reason I'm here. I care for no one else on this earth."

Eleven months and a mere ten pages later, Bruce left her, once and for all. Posy preserved his breakup note, written in red ink on graph paper. "Thank you for not calling," the letter begins. "They are back from Aruba," it continues, not indicating who "they" are—though Posy must have known. "And they say," he goes on, "I am Guilty of hurting you w/ my independence."

The gist is that Bruce was leaving her but couldn't do it in person, and so left a note.

Posy eventually met with him, on Easter, at which point he told her they had been together six years exactly. He said it was simply too long for him.

Several days later, she wrote, "I truly hope Bruce gets some counseling."

~

"A long weekend. My birthday weekend," begins another entry. "42 years old. Well, how will I fuck this one up? Last weekend was delivered, Federal Express, from Hell. And Hell was here on earth, in my house. What a frightful party we had."

The next entry:

And so I opened my door around 10am to start. And hopefully finish some errands. What I did not see or feel at that moment, was (were?) one, or several hundred angels stampeding over me. Crowding me out of my house, sitting on my head, shoulders, hanging on to my clothes...

But they are so light, you see, that you don't know they are there—

until later.

I have been blessed and encouraged!

I am so extraordinarily lucky

This day, the 1st of May, I will never forget.

I wish the angels wouldn't go—but, you know, to tell you the truth, their presence is *so* intense—

"I'm not in my body," she wrote a few lines later. Then, a few months and pages after that, "I will not be alive this time next year."

She began waking up at seven p.m. and going through her morning routine, thinking it was seven in the morning. She visited a friend at his home, and when he saw the "livid" bruises on her arms, made when she smacked them against the walls in her clumsy stupors, he sat her down and prayed for her. She told her therapist "I didn't want anymore help. Period. Passive suicide. Drinking. Smoking." Her doctor—"Dr. Strange"—told her she should be in a hospital. Others would soon tell her the same thing. "They will have to drag me kicking and screaming," she wrote.

And so they did. A sheet of looseleaf paper, stuck in the back of the diary, begins, "I'm in the Detox wing of Arlington Hospital. I cannot believe it. This is the last place I want to be. Anne + Noel brought me here at Potter's insistence." She was given valium every two hours; she hated the food; the other patients frightened her. But on another sheet of paper, dated nineteen days later, she wrote just three paragraphs about what a *"Community"* she and the other patients had built together, and how much she would miss them when she left.

Thanks to my parents' unwelcome interruption of her prolonged attempt at "passive suicide," Posy would live another sixteen-and-a-half years.

~

On a Saturday in June, my brother Jim cleaned his basement, with the help of our mother. From among the clutter she pulled a handful of papers that had belonged to Posy. She promptly mailed them to me, in the hope that I could use them for my book.

Two of the papers were letters written from Posy to herself.

"I'm so scared I don't know what to do," began the first. "I cannot see myself getting any older—don't want to die, but don't want to live—like *this*." As in so many entries in her diaries, she declares herself depressed. It was written a few months after her stay at Arlington, the revitalizing effects of which had worn off.

The next letter, written three years later, in 1996, is a response to the first one. She calls her prior letter "upsetting," and insists that she wouldn't recognize it as hers were it not in her handwriting. She is at one of her high points, a vantage from which she can question why she ever fell in with Bruce; where she recognizes that although her "'incarceration'" at Arlington left her thinking she would never drink again, as soon as summer arrived she knew how unlikely that was.

This point is made a little more strongly by Bruce, a couple of whose letters from late in their affair were included in the papers in Jim's basement. "You *have* a disease," he wrote her. "You are *not* capable of 'controlling' it, playing around the edges of it, 'sipping' a nip or 2 now & then........" The letter grows only more vehement as Bruce threatens a breakup. He gives my aunt three choices:

1. *Stop* stop Stop! (I'm not sure you can)

or   2. I'm outta here—(I cannot help you) + (I cannot bear to stay)

or   3. If I return, *find a better hiding place* for the vodka. That was quite a   volume, and...quite a lot of it *gone* in 3 days! (I saw the receipt—date)

That Posy kept her vodka receipts is simultaneously baffling and unsurprising; having been there to clean out her house when she died, I would be surprised if she ever threw out a receipt, no matter how incriminating it was.

Bruce concluded, in a postscript,

p.s.—The fish don't like it when U drink either, they *told* me so. So—I poured the rest of your stash into their *tank!* SHOCKED?! 'NO!' you say! 'It would kill them!' you say!

Well... It will kill you, too.
I poured it down the sink—but as Jay Leno says...
"Don't worry—they'll make more! All you have to do, is *Buy* it."
NOT!

It is like the first draft of the script of a radio play. But it speaks well on Bruce's behalf; I don't know what he said to her in person, but on this sheet of paper he did what he could to help her see what she was doing to herself. There is no record of Posy's reaction to it.

By the time these letters made their way to me in Missouri, I knew what it was that had killed my only aunt. I knew what had provoked her passive suicide. I suppose I had known it all along, but it was a knowledge that had defied language until then.

It wasn't something so easily pinpointed as her too-great enthusiasm for the contents of a bottle or a lifetime's worth of bad love. My recent understanding of Posy was one that bypassed the brain and went straight to the heart, out of which it could hardly be coaxed out and beaten into words.

Still, in pursuit of those words, having read Posy's journals, I traveled to Washington, D.C. I went with Stefanie to see the National Cathedral, the building Posy adored most in this world. "The Cathedral is a very special place for me," she wrote in 1990. "Every significant person in my life, since I moved here, has had a special memory for me involving the Cathedral." Its final stone had been placed just days before she wrote this entry, but she had missed the ceremony in favor of helping Bruce and his friend move into a new apartment.

I did not, like Posy, visit the Cathedral in order to pray there. I went to try to see in it what she had seen.

But it didn't fill me with the awe it filled her with. I couldn't picture her there. We must have passed the spot where she met Bruce—that NASA man who went to pick up women at a cathedral—but I couldn't have identified exactly where it was. The stained-glass windows were filled with what looked to me like figures from Disney cartoons.

Posy had walked the Cathedral with Lawrence, with me, with my brothers, sister and mother. She had loved this place, but as we ate breakfast, at a diner across the street, Stefanie and I agreed that we were unimpressed by the structure. I didn't say so, but I thought this building might be another thing Posy poured her heart into that didn't give quite enough back, even if she would have said differently.

In the last of Posy's diaries I read, the final entry was addressed to Bruce. She told him she was wearing a shirt he liked. "Damn," she wrote, "if it doesn't *smell* of you." Stuck between this page and the one before it is the blue pen she used to write the entry.

Its presence is an invitation to write more, or a sign of her intention to continue the journal. When I found it, it had been stuck there for almost twenty years. Its offer would not be taken up, not by the one who left it there.

~

When I learned, a year after Posy's death, that her house was to be sold to a lawyer with a family large enough to take up all its rooms, I was relieved—not because I cared if the rooms were occupied, but because I didn't want to think about the house anymore. Weeks would pass before the deal closed, but at last the home that had sat under the sun like an open wound for far too long would cease to weigh on my thoughts and my inheritance.

The house's problems were incessant, and so were its heating and cooling bills. They could be resolved only through the use of money taken from Posy's estate. So, as the house persisted unsold, my inheritance diminished by increments.

It was the principle of this that bothered me most, as the house had been the site of nothing less than some of Posy's greatest suffering. The stairway to the basement was not merely a stairway, but a site where Posy's blood had spilled. The yard was not just a handsome yard, but the setting in which Posy met Randall, where she had worked alongside him on the rare days he was willing to lift a finger, both of them usually drunk.

He told me about this behavior, once, as I sat with him and

Posy in her living room. He said, "I'm standing there watching her try to dig in a straight line and a minute later the line is just like this," and he illustrated with a sweep of his hand how the line was not straight at all. Posy looked on. No one laughed but Randall.

~

Soon after the deal on the house closed, the sword found its rightful place in our home at last—or, I finally took the trouble of hanging it on one of our walls. Above a pair of bookshelves it would suspend, I decided, from a couple of nails by fishing wire.

This was more than a matter of my finally having gotten around to accomplishing a mundane task. Hanging the sword meant something—it meant that in my house I would feature an emblem that stood for an untimely death. It would hang in the same room where Stefanie and I watched television, where we ate dinner and entertained guests.

When they came over, most of them made note of the new addition to our wall. If they didn't I pointed it out to them. For them, it was a thing to spend several seconds looking at.

For me it was—and is—a potentially dangerous metal thing that looks surprisingly nice up there on the wall and reminds me when I look at it of the fate that waits to greet me with arms open, or sword upraised, in case I choose to go and meet it.

I am not Posy's son, but many of her genes are still mine, and I like to drink. I don't like vodka, as Posy did; I drink beer and whiskey, much more often the former than the latter. I don't drink too much, but I drink, and I know that I could die alone in a bed in a house with poison coursing through me the way Posy did. The sword stands for the death that will be mine if I want it, and it hangs there, just behind and above my head.

I hung the sword at about the time that Posy's things began to lose their luster. I had not expected it to happen, and I should have. About a year after she died, it was as if someone overturned each of her former things and poured out its significance.

It started with her records.

At first I had been reluctant to let go of her Donovan collection, her Steeleye Span, and her many albums by Paul Revere and the

171

Raiders. I never listened to them, but they had been hers, and they were precious for a while.

At some uncertain point, I no longer felt like clinging to these things I didn't use. I sold them off, for next-to-nothing.

Soon I found I had filled my home with dozens of heavy artifacts that meant little to me, and I recalled the advice Stefanie offered on the day I made my list of new acquisitions at Posy's house. "You should take just a few things," she had urged me. "Take one valuable thing, and one thing that reminds you of her, and then maybe something you think you'll use at home. That's all you need."

I had ignored her outright.

It took me a year to see how right she'd been. Not all of my inheritance is as easily cast off as the records; I am much more reluctant to sell a family heirloom like the vase in our kitchen. But I don't necessarily want to own it, either. It sits there, in plain sight, and it will be there until it breaks or I do.

~

Spring returned, as usual. It was the second spring since 1950 that Posy would not be present for.

I was sitting up late one night in my Missouri living room, alone, when out of nowhere I smelled her perfume. I don't know how to describe the smell—it must have been the simulated fragrance of a flower I don't know the name of—but it was unmistakably hers. I had never smelled it anywhere other than with her, and I haven't smelled it since.

Like that fleeting odor, with the new season came memories of Posy that had been buried under grief, or the need to get on with life, or whatever it was that they had lain buried under since she'd died.

I remembered how Posy cried as I boarded the bus to Wheeling, at the end of my first-ever visit to her in D.C., when I was seventeen. I had with me the big, blue duffel bag I kept under my bed, at home. It was always stuffed with some essential supplies, in case I finally found the courage to escape the house I was raised in and never come back.

When I returned home to Wheeling, I went to sleep, and when I awoke my mother stood over me, holding a plastic bag full of green leaves of an herb she didn't recognize. She asked what it was. I knew at once what she thought it was, but it was rosemary. Posy had given it to me, to give to my mother, but I had forgotten it and left it in one of the bag's blue pockets.

Many of my visits to Posy in D.C. had taken place in spring. I don't know why; I suppose it was the time of year that made me most restless and eager to escape my childhood and adolescent home. I never did find the courage to steal away in the night with my duffel bag, so I settled for trips to see Posy, underwritten by my parents.

I accompanied her often on her morning commute to work. I saw her office, saw Lawrence there and their self-effacing Haitian colleague, Dionne. As Posy worked all day, I went out, and rambled through the Mall, gaping at monuments.

I remembered a festival put on by the Smithsonian. It was a hot day, when we went to see it. I drank a smoothie to cool off, but got an ice cream headache that came on so swiftly and so painfully that I ran under a tent, crouched as if bracing for a mortar impact, and began crying. Then I laughed at myself, and Posy laughed, too.

We went to another tent, to watch a voodoo ceremony. I don't remember the voodoo ceremony.

~

As if to flaunt their ability to emerge from the ground long after they are put under it, members of a local species of cicada returned to the surface of Missouri after thirteen years spent living in the earth.

For those who have not been initiated to them, cicadas are flying insects, each one the size of a thumb, that spend nearly their whole lives underground—thirteen years for some, seventeen for others. When they emerge, they do so in such numbers that one cannot walk outside without them grabbing onto clothes and skin. For the weeks they spend in the open, they do as much of four activities as they can: chew trees, lay eggs, mate, and die.

I knew they were coming a month in advance, when I saw the cicada-sized holes in my front lawn. Under the tree, in the yard, where hardly a blade of grass grew, the earth opened one pore at a time. Then, as if in response to a cue only they could hear, the creatures erupted one morning, filling the air, filling the trees, flying here and there like drunken bumblebees in red goggles and ill-fitting suits, landing on whatever they could, including my arms, hair, legs, and wife. When I swatted them away, they screeched like injured dogs. They smelled like the worst part of the forest, especially when they started dying, their bodies piling up on every lawn.

Stefanie and I were absent for their first appearance, as we had taken a trip to Wheeling to see my parents. The insects had spared Wheeling; we didn't encounter them until we made the drive west through Illinois. At some uncertain point, we noticed that just above the noise of the highway and the car we could hear the rolling screech of cicadas.

It was to be our constant soundtrack for weeks to come—a high-pitched, pulsating scream they produced in unison. It rose and fell like the sound of waves breaking and receding at the shore of an ocean on a planet far away from this one.

It was not my first encounter with hordes of cicadas. In my senior year of high school, in Wheeling, the seventeen-year cicadas had erupted from the ground and ruined my summer. For a month I couldn't go anywhere without them harassing me. When I went out in the day I carried a flyswatter, inspired by my friend Karen, a lifeguard who, for as long as the plague lasted, kept a tennis racket with her when she worked. At night the creatures slept on the sidewalk, so that on my long walks in the dark, which I had been taking habitually for years, I had to dodge them as carefully as I could or else my stroll would be a massacre.

Partly in order to escape the cicadas, I made another visit to see Posy.

Imagine my disappointment when I found that cicada territory stretched all the way to D.C. There were as many filling the air at the capitol as there were in my provincial home.

Unable to resist the materials presented her, Posy made from Styrofoam a small head, meant to be that of a young woman, her hair made from the discarded wings of dead cicadas.

~

I remember that once when I joined Posy for her commute to work in downtown D.C., she pulled us over to where some men and women stood in suits, on the sidewalk, waiting—for what I could not tell. Turning to me, she said, "Lean your head out the window and say, 'Bops.'"

I didn't understand why someone would ever want to do that, so I looked at her with my mouth open. We were stopped beside the suited men and women. Some were looking at me expectantly. Posy had rolled down my window. "Say 'Bops,'" she ordered again. I stammered. I started to ask her what in the world that would mean for me, when she leaned across my side of the car and shouted, "Bops!"

One of the men climbed into the back of the car, and we were off.

Later the same week, I returned with Posy to her townhouse after a long walk, when she stopped abruptly, pointed at the wall, and said, "Wall!" I laughed because I thought she was clowning, but still she pointed. "Wall," she said more urgently than before. Her cat was on the stairs nearby, so I thought she was asking me to say "Wall" to the cat as some form of discipline. So I turned to Angel and said, "Wall." Posy sighed, took a magazine from her kitchen table, and used it to smack a moth off her wall, one that had been right in front of my face, but which I had not seen.

There were moths infesting her house that Spring, I remembered. We were killing them all the time, and there were always more.

~

The cicada explosion brought death to Missouri. Death is always in Missouri, of course, just as it is everywhere, but rarely is it so present as it was in the cicada spring. Everywhere I went, a cicada was dead, being killed, or on its way to a mushy end. I couldn't pull my car out of the driveway without murdering a handful, as they had an unwise affection for clinging to the treads of my tires.

It would have been easy to be cruel to the insects. They had no means to defend themselves.

I could have crushed them with my shoes and hands, or put neglected books to use again by dropping them on cicadas, but I never went that far.

The only thing worse than a live cicada is one being killed. They are quick to whine and scream, and when crushed they produce a sound I associate with Raisin Bran.

I avoided hurting them as fervently as I avoided touching them. I didn't go near them when I could help it, and it was rare that I could. Every tree swarmed with cicadas. They would cling there for a while and then, at some arbitrary moment, fly away from the tree in order to land on another tree. Anything that stood vertically was likely to be mistaken for a tree, even if it moved, especially if it was a person. A quick walk to the library became a pest-ridden obstacle course, as I did everything I could to dodge or—if necessary—smack them away. The only ones who seemed to be as wary of the cicadas as I was were pre-teenage girls.

~

Posy was funny, and she could use her good humor to end conversations. I was fighting with my mother in her kitchen, once, about something frivolous enough that I don't remember it. Posy pointed to a button on the microwave that read "Clear / Off" and told me, "Clear off!" She was telling me to shut up and leave the room, but with charm. I laughed, and left the room.

On the Thanksgiving before Posy died, we gathered in my parents' living room to play a game the name of which I don't remember. It came in a box and worked like the dictionary game, except that it involved sayings and aphorisms rather than individual words. Someone would draw a card with a common expression written on it, and each player would have to come up with a fake explanation for how it came to be. The object was to fool the others. If you fooled the others you got points, the number of points to be determined by the other players.

I didn't like this game, because I don't like games that involve voting or anything like it.

I would have simply not played, but someone would have harangued me for my refusal to participate and be a part of the family. So I played.

If I remember correctly, I was tasked with pretending to explain the phrase "roughing it." I was supposed to come up with something that sounded convincing. My written explanation is irrecoverable, but because I couldn't take the game seriously I wrote in such a convoluted way that no one could possibly believe it was real, or an earnest attempt at sounding real. So on her last Thanksgiving, in my parents' living room, Posy read my "roughing it" explanation aloud. She did a wonderful job, and if I remember right it had the desired effect of sabotaging the game, which everyone soon quit playing.

It occurs to me, now, that that was the only thing I wrote that Posy ever read.

~

One night early in the cicada outbreak, some of my friends had a party on their back patio. I was reluctant to attend, for I predicted with great accuracy what would happen. At first the cicadas were willing to mind their own business, but as it grew dark the patio light attracted them. They smacked their heads against it like amateur moths. They fell in and could not get back out. They clung to my hosts' kitchen door, and a persistent few were able to make their way in through a crack in its screen. There they encountered the two resident cats, Noodle and Zipper, who knocked them over.

Cicadas are pitifully unable to right themselves, once they have been put on their backs. Occasionally one will flutter its wings and flip itself right-side-up, but this solution eludes most of them. At one point I walked into the house to find three live ones wagging back and forth against the floor, as Zipper crunched another one in his jaws and Noodle watched.

Back on the patio, my friends invoked unsolicited cicada facts. Camellia said, when she first noticed how much I hated and was frightened by the insects, "They'll only hurt you if they think you're a tree and try to take a bite out of you. It almost never happens." Someone else mentioned, when contemplating a meal of cicadas, "The females are supposed to be meatier than the males."

What interested me about the cicadas was not their culinary potential but the plainness of what I perceived to be their evolutionary wisdom. I know there really isn't such a thing, as evolution is random and not wise, but I admired how the cicadas were so stupid, clumsy and useless, but managed to survive by exposing themselves to predators for a mere few weeks every thirteen years. They are no good at dodging their killers; throughout the spring I watched birds, fish and cats eat them without even having to work for it. But they couldn't eat all of the cicadas, and that was the point. When a species survives by virtue of sheer numbers, it means almost nothing when one of its members dies abruptly.

~

The last visit I ever made to Posy was in her final summer, when she was living in Wheeling. I stopped there with Stefanie for a few days. We went to Posy's house, where Stefanie met her for the first—only—time. I recall nothing from our conversation—only that Randall was absent, and that Posy, who had met several of my previous girlfriends, none of whom I married, seemed to like Stefanie. Posy was, or seemed to be, sober.

In the morning, as we prepared to drive back to Missouri, she intercepted us. We had retrieved some furniture from my parents' basement, a couple of chairs they had kept there for years but no longer sat in. The chairs were big and awkward, and wouldn't fit into my little Civic. As we made our fifth or sixth attempt at jamming them in, Posy rolled up in her Corolla, sprung out of it, and asked what I was doing. Something was wrong, and I couldn't place what it was.

She said something to me that I don't remember. I do recall that it was an incredibly mean thing to say, the sort of thing I had never heard her say before, the kind of thing I might say to a cicada. It would hurt me still if I could recall it, but for reasons I can't explain I tend to forget quickly the exact content of insults, despite how long the pain they cause can last. I was in a state of mild shock as Stefanie and I continued our struggle with the furniture, and Posy made her way across the street to my parents' door.

We never fit the chair into the car. As we drove off, finally, it dawned on me what state I had just seen Posy in. For nearly thirty years I had known her but had never seen her drunk. Now I had and wished I hadn't.

If I had my memories under control, I would make that one disappear.

178

I didn't think to recognize Posy's public stupor as a sign of anything other than merely what it was. I did not see its significance. Posy was slipping, losing what command of herself she had left.

She would live just another four months. We would never meet again.

~

By the middle of June, the last of Missouri's cicadas were dying off, leaving the stink of their corpses behind them. Their bodies littered the city. All that was left of most of them were two wings stuck together with nothing between them. The holes they had made in my front lawn would remain for weeks like open graves, but soon I found I could walk through the town freely, without fear of being made a landing pad for something horrid. I could step anywhere I wanted without first looking where my foot landed to see if an innocent thing lay there.

Surely, in the weeks of their aboveground visitation, I stepped on a cicada or two—or two dozen, or more—without knowing it. With the probability of this in mind, I had for weeks worn boots heavy enough that I would not feel the cicadas' bodies being crushed as I smashed them by mistake. If I killed insects by walking on them, I didn't want to know. I avoided it as best I could.

Despite my hatred for them, I was determined not to harm the cicadas. But as I walked into a wine bar, a few drinks into one late spring night, I set my foot on the pavement to hear the wet, unmistakable crunch I had tried so diligently to steer myself away from. Under my foot was a flattened, harmless monster with its insides spilled out on the sidewalk like pus seeping out of an infected wound.

~

It was not until after Posy's death, when I began receiving pieces of her estate, that the inheritance I would leave the next generation felt in any way real to me, when I began dreaming on a semi-nightly basis about an infant child whom I could not seem to properly take care of. In every dream I would lose the baby, drop it, or leave it somewhere and not come back for many hours, only to remember it later and realize I had

179

murdered it with my absent mind.

The infants in my dreams were even more fragile than real babies. They were no larger than the palms of my hands on some nights, and they never had faces. Some were made of clay, but wept when I pulled their arms too hard and tore them apart without meaning to.

It was hard to think seriously about the generation to come, when this was how it was portrayed so often in my sleep. It was hard not to be afraid of my prospective children, who were bound to be fragile and helpless, physically for at least a few years, and financially for many more.

I knew that when they finally came there would be nothing I could do to make them more physically resilient, but Posy managed, by dying, to make more probable such things as their college educations.

Her money arrived as checks in the mail, in a series of installments, the sum increasing with each increment. As they made the trip to rendezvous with my mailbox, halfway across the country, taking probably the same route I took when hauling Posy's objects to Missouri, I wondered what in the world I would do with the money.

I dreamed up costly irresponsibilities. I could buy three cars, twenty suits and a big television. I could keep some hidden at home, in cash, in a suitcase, in case I had to flee in the night. I could buy a shotgun.

I talked about the money with Stefanie, who was also made nervous by the thought of it. In the scheme of things it wasn't that much money, we agreed, but the fact of it arriving all at once made it seem gargantuan. It was just enough to make a poor couple of newlyweds swoon.

I admitted to Stefanie that it would feel different if we'd worked for the money, if we'd done something to warrant having it, like if one of us had written a successful erotic romance novel. It would seem, then, like we were entitled to the money. But instead we were simply lucky, and our luck was embarrassing.

~

"I bequeath myself to the dirt to grow from the grass I love," wrote Walt Whitman, famously, urging us to see more than grass in grass, more than a cicada in a cicada. "If you want me look for me under your boot-soles."

If I am to see Whitman under my shoes, then surely I can look for Posy there, too.

But perhaps it would be more pertinent to say that I see Posy under my boot-soles when I stand in my house. It is Posy who will help to keep me and my boot-soles there, if I go broke, because she put me in her will and I thus have a savings, and can continue to pay the rent if I lose my job. As much as Posy might have liked to dwell in the grass like Whitman—or, even better, in her garden—it is in her former belongings that I'll look for her.

Like the weight of her memory, I bear with me her drawings, photographs and other material things, and so I will continue to do until my time comes to join her. Then it will be someone else's turn.

~

Planning to father a child as I was, I found that I worried, more and more, and not always for absurd reasons, about the threat of apocalypse, or partial apocalypse. Conventional wisdom suggested we'd been inviting it for more than a century, with the ice caps melting and the acid ocean encroaching further onto land. But even those worries seem old-fashioned to me now, as the weather systems inspired by climate change feel far more imminently catastrophic than any other symptoms of a dying world.

Films depicting the end of the human race look ever more accurate to the future I almost expect to live to see. I find—in all seriousness—that I am worried less about death than I am about the possibility that I will live long enough to see the potential—probable?—horrors of the 21st century's second half.

I don't doubt that in every generation there are those who feel this way, who wonder how they can bring children into a world that seems to diminish before their eyes and slowly take its people with it. My worries are not exactly new. I tell myself this, but it doesn't help me to shake the impression that I am living on the cusp of something awful.

I would like to see inheritance change its shape, and become something that benefits everyone rather than a select few. We could all start taking inheritance seriously, as something that belongs to everyone, rather than as something to be handed down from one individual to a handful of people or fewer.

I expect instead for my children, or their children, to witness a time when inherited things, like portraits and silver flatware, become truly valueless, when it becomes not only frivolous but unfeasible to keep them, when my inheritors are so completely at the mercy of forces beyond their control that they must cast off their material histories in an effort to survive their futures.

It occurred to me, as I entertained these thoughts, that if Stefanie and I lived out our lives without having children, then we could inhabit the world with a vague sense of abandon. If things got truly terrible, then we could die, and that would be it. But if we brought another person into our equation, then we might have wronged her unforgivably, and damned the world with one more body to sustain.

This kind of thinking is merciless, but such cold calculations seem more necessary with every piece of bad news I read. I wouldn't want to curse someone with life at a time when living, in the fullest sense of the word, is less and less tenable.

~

Even as I renewed these thoughts daily, our plans to have a child grew only more certain. Soon there were no birth control pills in our house, where before there had been birth control pills. A basal thermometer replaced them, and a few months later Stefanie came to me in bed one morning, holding in her hand a small white stick with a plus sign on it.

~

As if to confirm my perception of our family, as if to substantiate all that I had written about the lineage our son or daughter would be born into, my mother—when I told her about the conception—immediately sent me a spoon made of sterling silver.

She had had the spoon for years, she said. She had forgotten about it. But when I informed her that in some months she would have a third grandchild, the presence of the spoon in her house once again crossed her mind.

It is a small spoon—a baby spoon. As if to better announce the age group of its intended user, at the top of the spoon is the image of the head of a small child, in profile, with flowing hair.

Engraved on the underside of the spoon is the full name of my grandfather, as is a date—12-25-12—signifying his first Christmas, on which it was given to him. It was one of his first belongings ever, and, as my mother explained, he gave it to me soon after I was born. Written beside his name is my name, with the date of my birth engraved underneath.

My mother sent me the spoon so I could use it to feed my child mushy peas when he or she is old enough to eat them. But of course there was more to it than that.

On the spoon's handle, on the side opposite the side with my name and my grandfather's, is a space for the name of someone who did not yet exist. "NAME," the spoon prompts, with a blank space underneath those capital letters. Beside that it reads, "BORN," and beside that, "WEIGHT," with other spaces where the next child's stats are to be recorded.

Several things about the spoon unsettled me, starting with the fact that for the past thirty years there'd been a spoon in this world with my name on it, and I didn't know. All this time, I thought the only things that had my name on them—at least in reference to me and not someone who shares my name—were tax forms, my driver's license, my social security card, certain web sites, and a couple of other things. Eventually, a headstone might make the list, and, perhaps, copies of this book. I never thought a spoon would join the company of these things, but there it was in my hands, in Missouri.

When he had the spoon engraved, my grandfather had parts of it left blank, and for a reason. He was leaving space for the name of my child.

The oncoming birth of my child, in other words, was anticipated starting the day I was born.

By having a child, I am doing exactly what has been expected of me. By producing—with Stefanie—another person, I am presenting to the world another vehicle for the spoon, and my grandparents' wedding silver, and the glassware, and the books I have collected, and the sword.

My child will be here to have a good life, I hope, and to do the things a human being does. She will also keep the wheels of inheritance spinning. She will receive things she didn't ask for, things she may not even want.

I wonder what in the world she will do with it all.

JIGSAW PUZZLE

We started with the edges, digging for them where they lay buried among other pieces in the big cardboard box that David had brought home for Christmas. We took turns sifting through pieces, until we started dividing them by color into big, ceramic bowls.

Half of solving a jigsaw puzzle is sorting the pieces. It is, at least, when the puzzle is a 9,000-piece reproduction of Hieronymus Bosch's 15th century triptych *The Garden of Earthly Delights*. Being a triptych, it has three panels, and each one looks different enough from the next: Adam, God and Eve on the left; middle panel of earthly delights; Hell on the right.

We assembled the puzzle on the biggest table in my mother's house, in a room where, early last century, she said, a wake would have been held.

We weren't having a wake. We don't mourn at my mother's house—not formally. There had been a funeral for Miles, David's son, when he died four months prior, but at my mother's house we do things like puzzles, as we sit by the fireplace and talk about dogs. I drink beer.

As we worked through the first day, Stefanie, pregnant with our second daughter, wandered in a few times to put some pieces in place. Moriah, our first daughter, stood on a chair and scattered to the floor all the pieces she could reach with her little arms, for no reason. I took her away.

On the second day, some of our cousins came to help with the puzzle. Sue helped. Maggie helped. Chess came and assembled half the ferns on the left-hand panel before he had to go. Mostly, though, it was David and I who sat hunched over the big table in the room where we were not having a wake.

We hunched for hours. My neck hurt.

I don't know what Bosch meant the whole triptych to do or say, but the intent of the right-hand panel seems plain, depicting as it does the torments that lie in wait for sinners like me (I like beer too much) when they die. If you're not careful, then in the next life you might be swallowed and excreted by a man-bird. You might get attacked by dogs.

I had no trouble putting together the man who was crucified on the strings of a harp, presumably for having enjoyed music. The parts most readily solved, it seemed, were the human figures looming big in Hell's foreground. A hand's got to connect to an arm, after all, a leg to a foot.

But for every puzzle piece that had a human face or foot on it, which made it locatable on the triptych, at least five had nothing on them but a solid color. There was pale, green grass and pale, blue sky—lots of both—and for a busy puzzle an expanse of solid black took up an awful lot of Hell.

There must have been 800 pieces of darkness visible. I tried assembling it. I didn't get far. Before long, I was staggered by the sheer emptiness of Bosch's Hell. That was the whole idea, and as I lost myself in the Hell of the right-hand panel I thought that if our grief were a jigsaw puzzle it might be the shattered windshield of Miles's RAV4, the pieces of which wouldn't stick together even if you could gather them all from the side of the road in Pennsylvania where his car leapt off the road, we don't know why.

You could never finish the grief puzzle, no matter who came to help solve it.

We thought we could do the Bosch puzzle in five days, if we put our minds to it. On the third day, though, we faced a harsh truth. The table where we had assembled not even a quarter of the puzzle so far wasn't big enough to hold the finished thing. We'd measured it, prior to starting. We'd measured wrong. The puzzle, when assembled, would be six feet long—man-sized. The table wasn't man-sized. There were no man-sized tables in the house.

We were not about to put the puzzle on the floor.

Our enthusiasm flagged. By the fourth day, no one was entering the room with the puzzle in it anymore.

It would go unsolved. The middle panel's revelers, with their enormous strawberries, would not be joined, through interlocking cardboard fragments, with the birds, pond, tower of gold and city aflame.

On the fifth day, we prepared to go our separate ways, but on our way out the door our mother promised it wasn't over. She meant the puzzle. She would buy card tables, she said. She would push them together, and lay the puzzle out on them. She would finish it herself, if we didn't come back.

ACKNOWLEDGMENTS

Thank you to John D'Agata, the contest judge, and Kathryn Nuern-berger and everyone at Pleiades Press who brought this book into the world. For helping to make this book worth bringing into the world, thank you to Maureen Stanton, Alexandra Socarides, and E.J. Levy. Thank you to Mark Brazaitis, Christopher Vyce, Paul Jones, and Rich-ard Rodriguez, for your insight and encouragement.

This book would not be what it is without a generous fellowship from the Virginia Center for the Creative Arts.

The essays in this collection first appeared in the following publications:

"Speak, Walking Stick" in *The Massachusetts Review*
"Clubs" in *Pleiades*
"Carlo" in the *American Literary Review*
"Dirty Laundry" in *Fourth Genre*
"Pigs and Eggplants" in *Alimentum*
"Guts" in *The Cossack Review*
"The Most Lifelike Thing in the Room" in *Michigan Quarterly Review*
"Boxes" in *Third Coast*.
"James and the Giant Noise Violation" in *The Journal*
"Skillet" in *Southern Indiana Review* as "My Skillet and I are Disappear-ing"
"Jigsaw Puzzle" in *River Teeth*.

Thank you to the editors of these publications, who have given my work their time, attention, and confidence. Thank you to those at *Best American Essays* who have included four of these essays on their annual lists of "Notable Essays."

Thank you to the family I came from and the family I've helped create: Stefanie, for her constant support and love; and Rose and Moriah, for putting stickers on me and taking me to the zoo.

Thank you to my friends, for being such good friends. There are too many of you to name.

ABOUT THE AUTHOR

Robert Long Foreman's essays and short stories have appeared in *Agni*, *Copper Nickel*, *The Cincinnati Review*, and the *Utne Reader*, among other publications. He has won a Pushcart Prize and the hearts of his wife and daughters. He lives with them in Kansas City.

THE ROBERT C. JONES PRIZE FOR PROSE

Robert C. Jones was a professor of English at University of Central Missouri and an editor at Mid-American Press who supported and encouraged countless young writers throughout a lifetime of editing and teaching. His legacy continues to inspire all of us who live, write, and support the arts in mid-America.

The editors at Plciades Press select 10-15 finalists from among those mnauscripts submitted each year. A judge of national renown selects one winner for publication.

ALSO AVAILABLE FROM PLEIADES PRESS

Book of No Ledge by Nance Van Winckel

Landscape with Headless Mama by Jennifer Givhan

Random Exorcisms by Adrian C. Louis

Poetry Comics from the Book of Hours by Bianca Stone

The Belle Mar by Katie Bickham

Sylph by Abigail Cloud

The Glacier's Wake by Katy Didden

Paradise, Indiana by Bruce Snider

What's this, Bombardier? by Ryan Flaherty

Self-Portrait with Expletives by Kevin Clark

Pacific Shooter by Susan Parr

It was a terrible cloud at twilight by Alessandra Lynch

Compulsions of Silkworms & Bees by Julianna Baggott

Snow House by Brian Swann

Motherhouse by Kathleen Jesme

Lure by Nils Michals

The Green Girls by John Blair

A Sacrificial Zinc by Matthew Cooperman

The Light in Our House by Al Maginnes

Strange Wood by Kevin Prufer